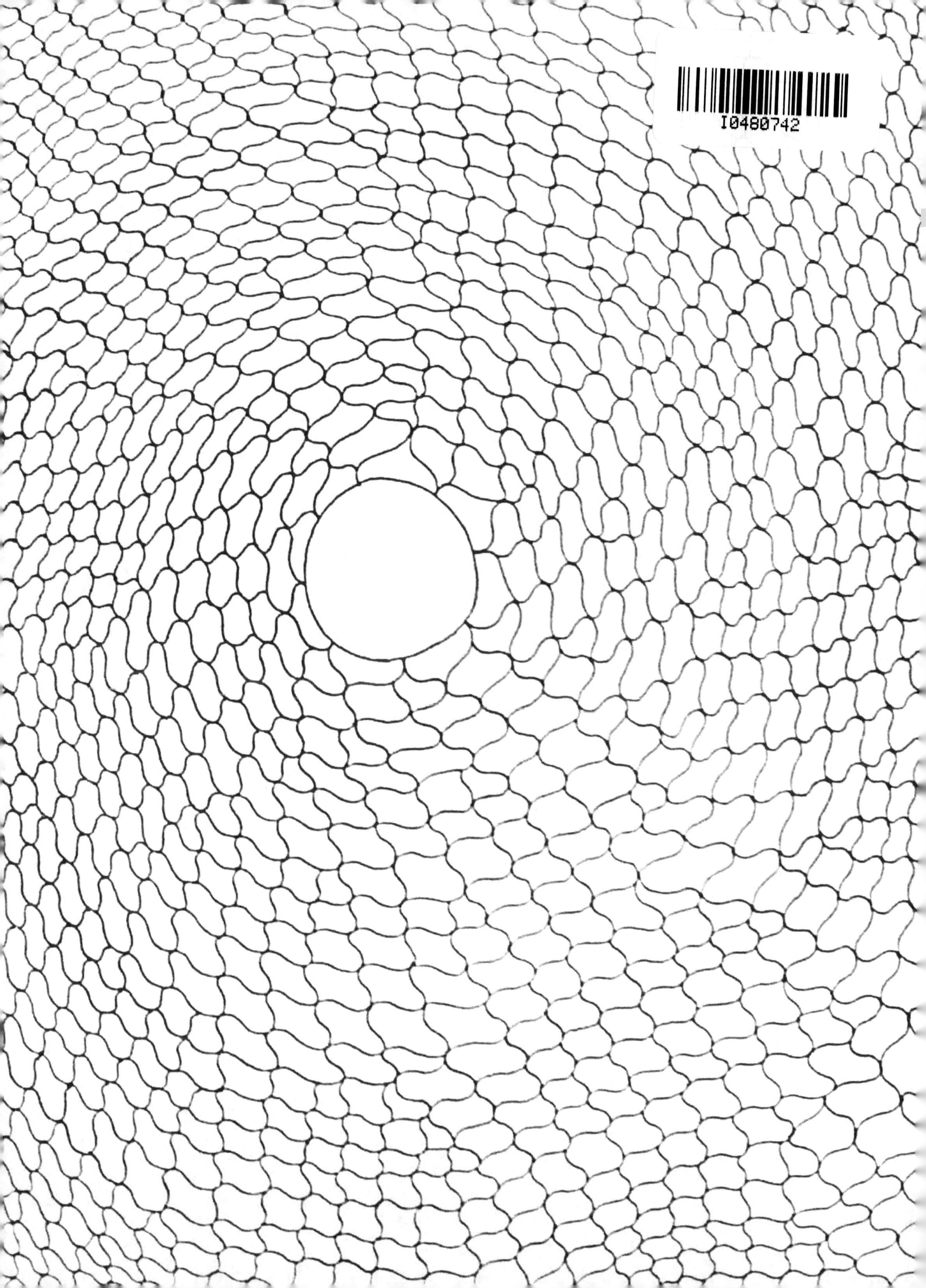

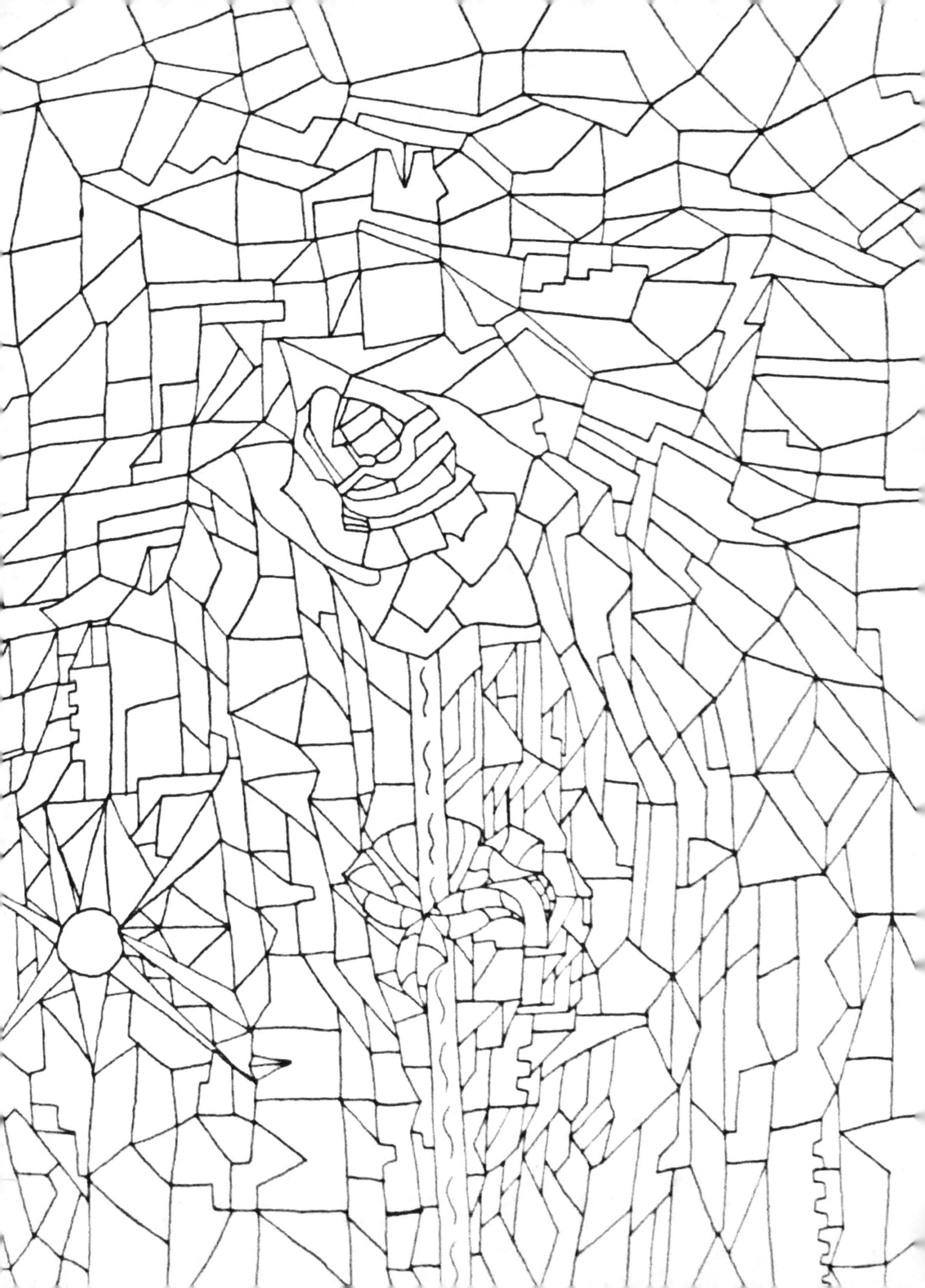

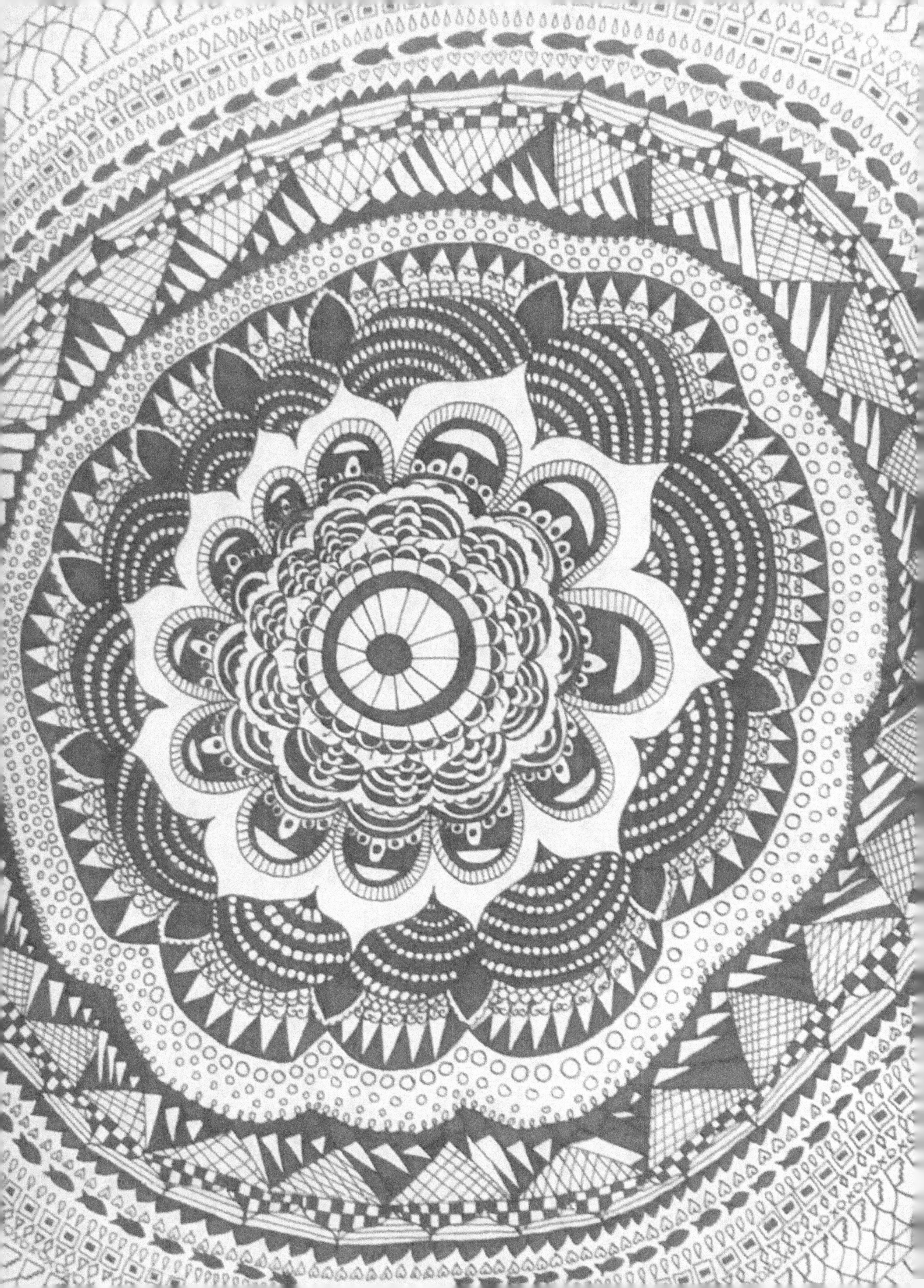

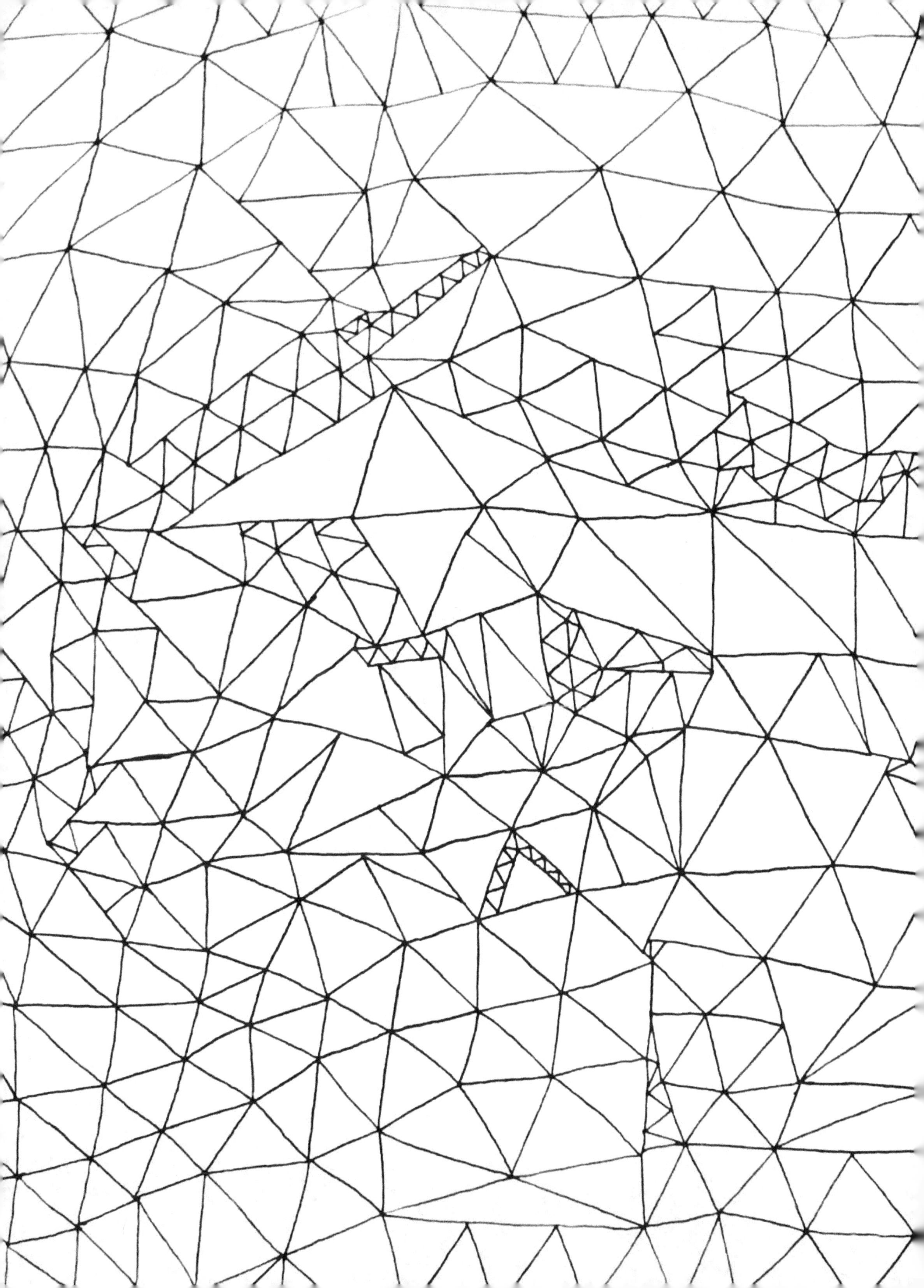

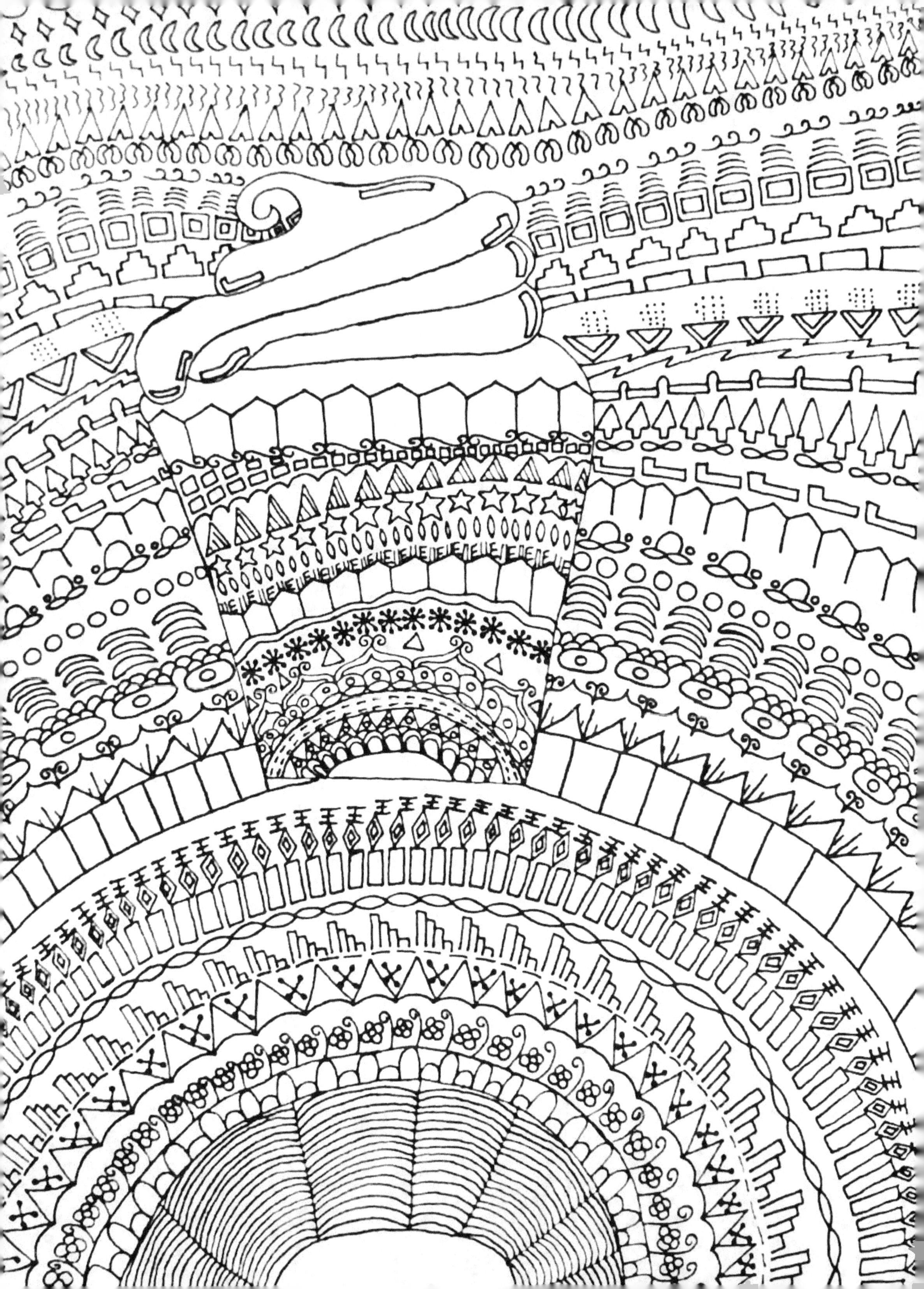

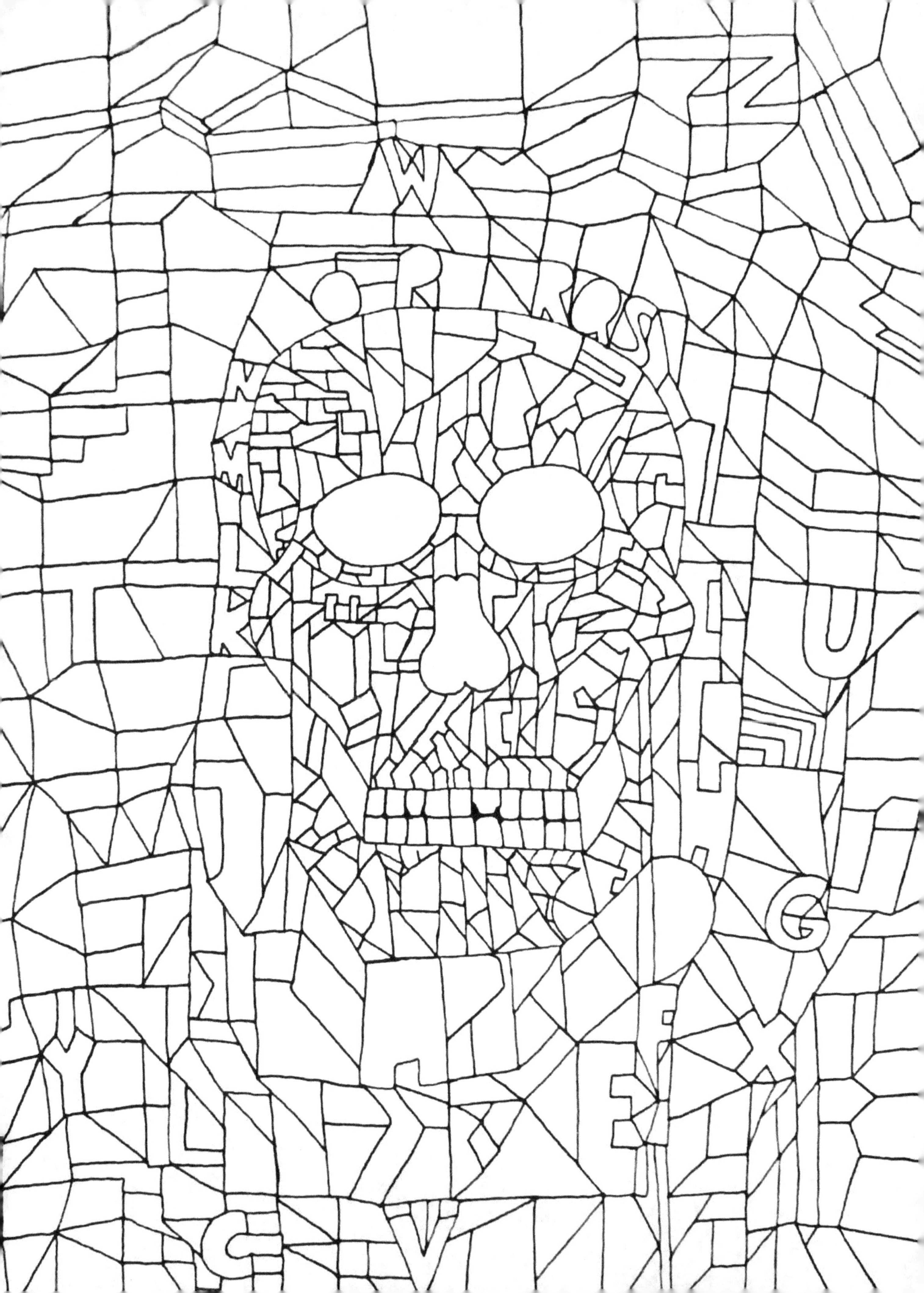

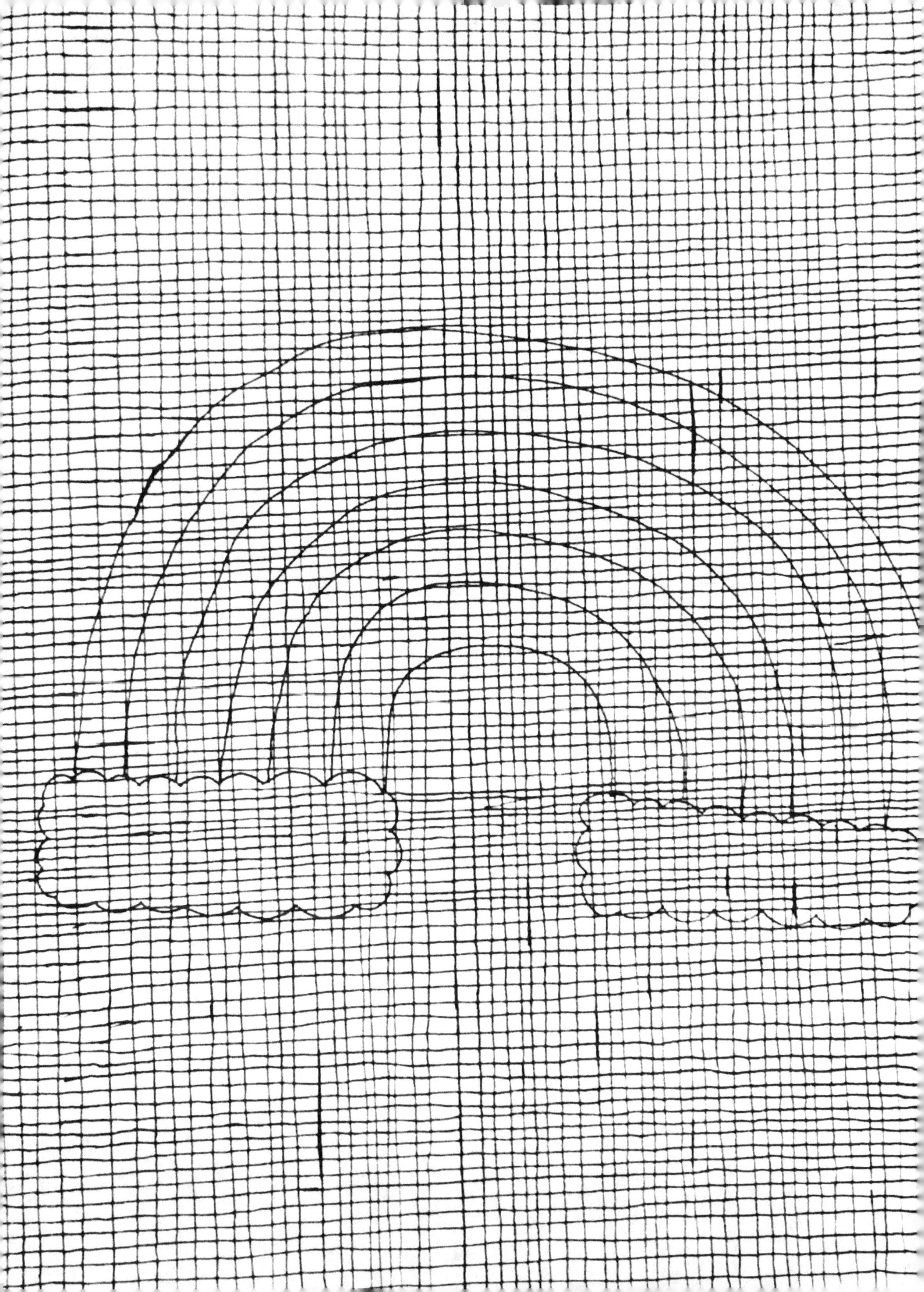

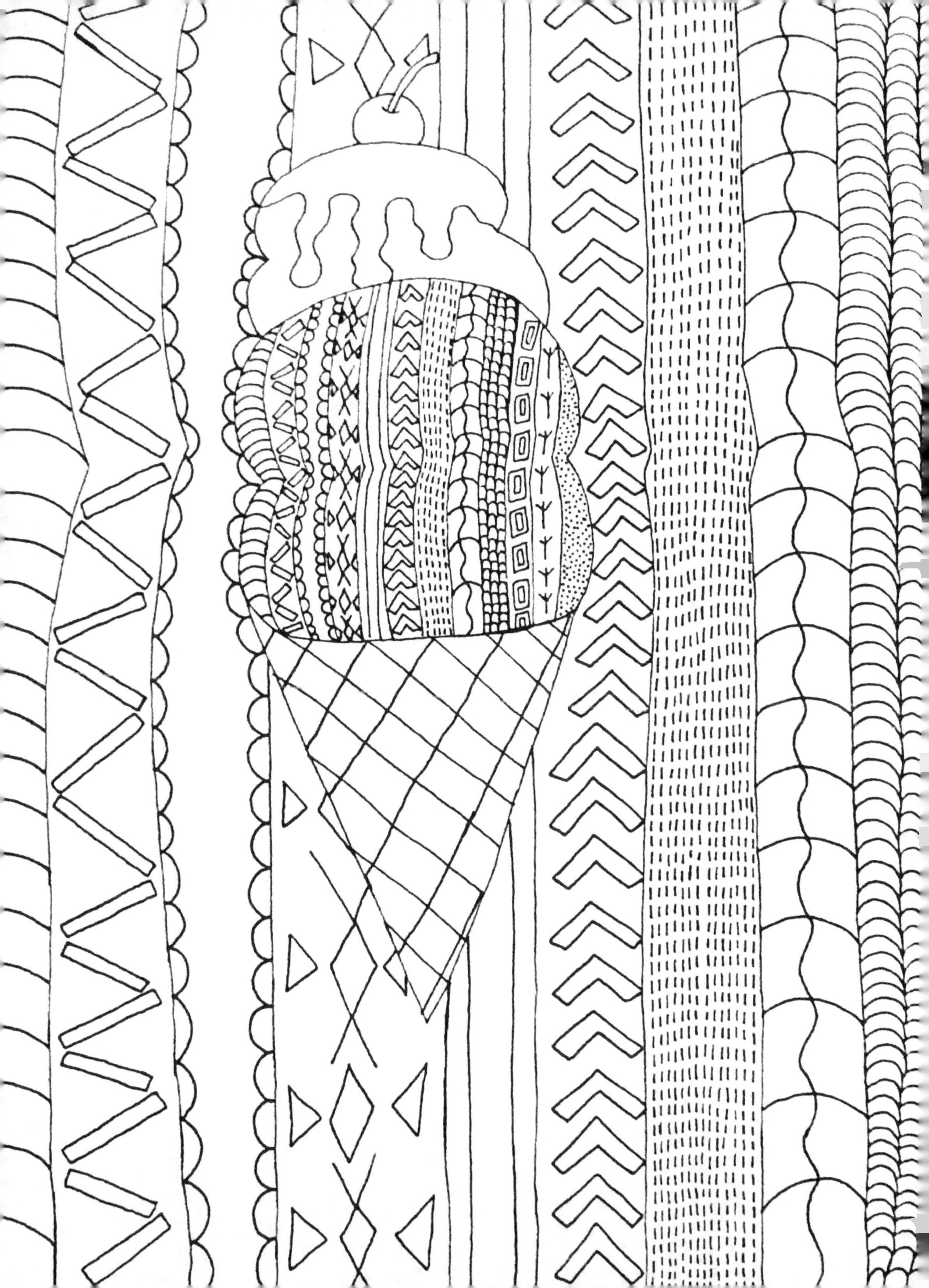

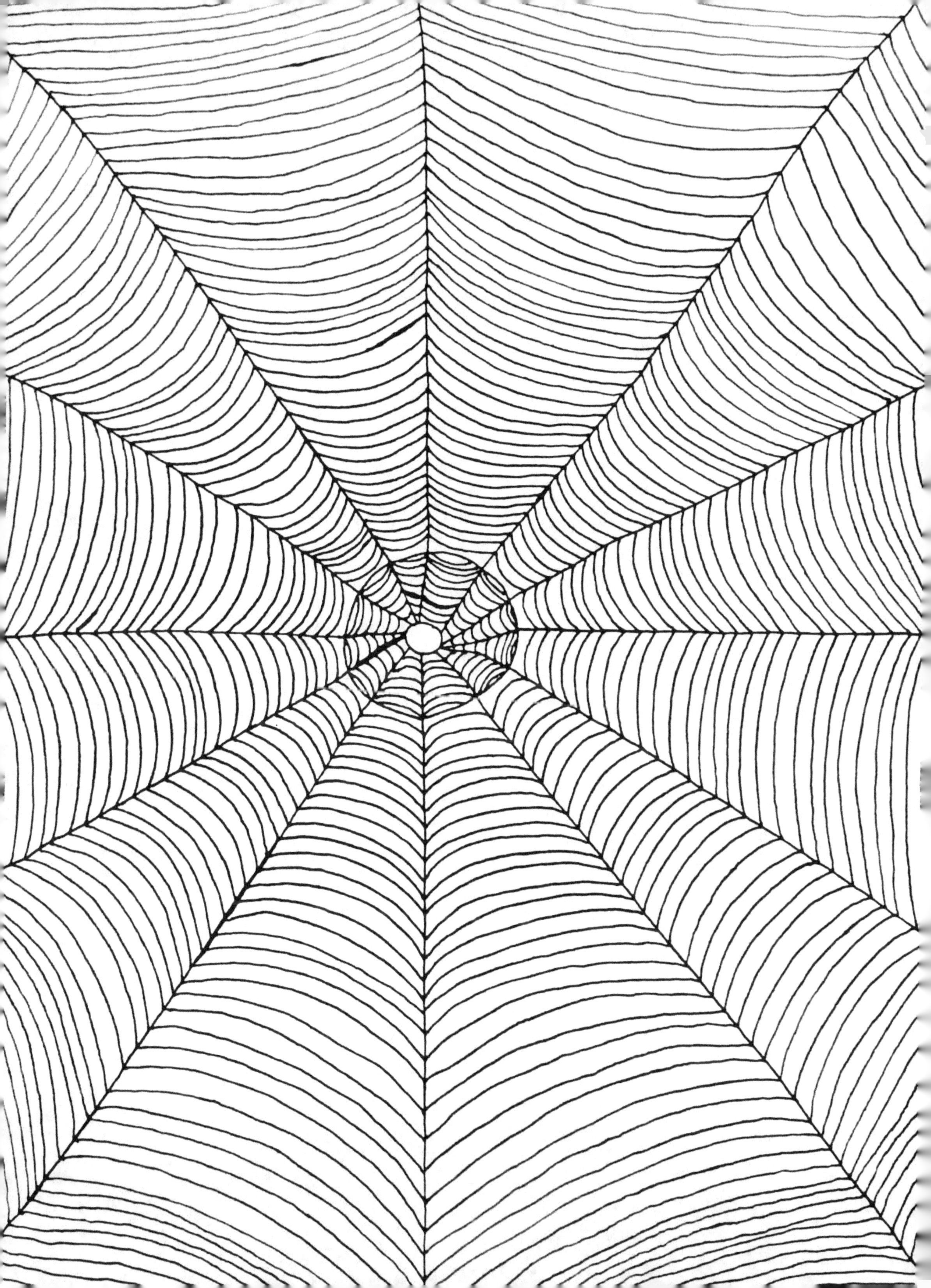

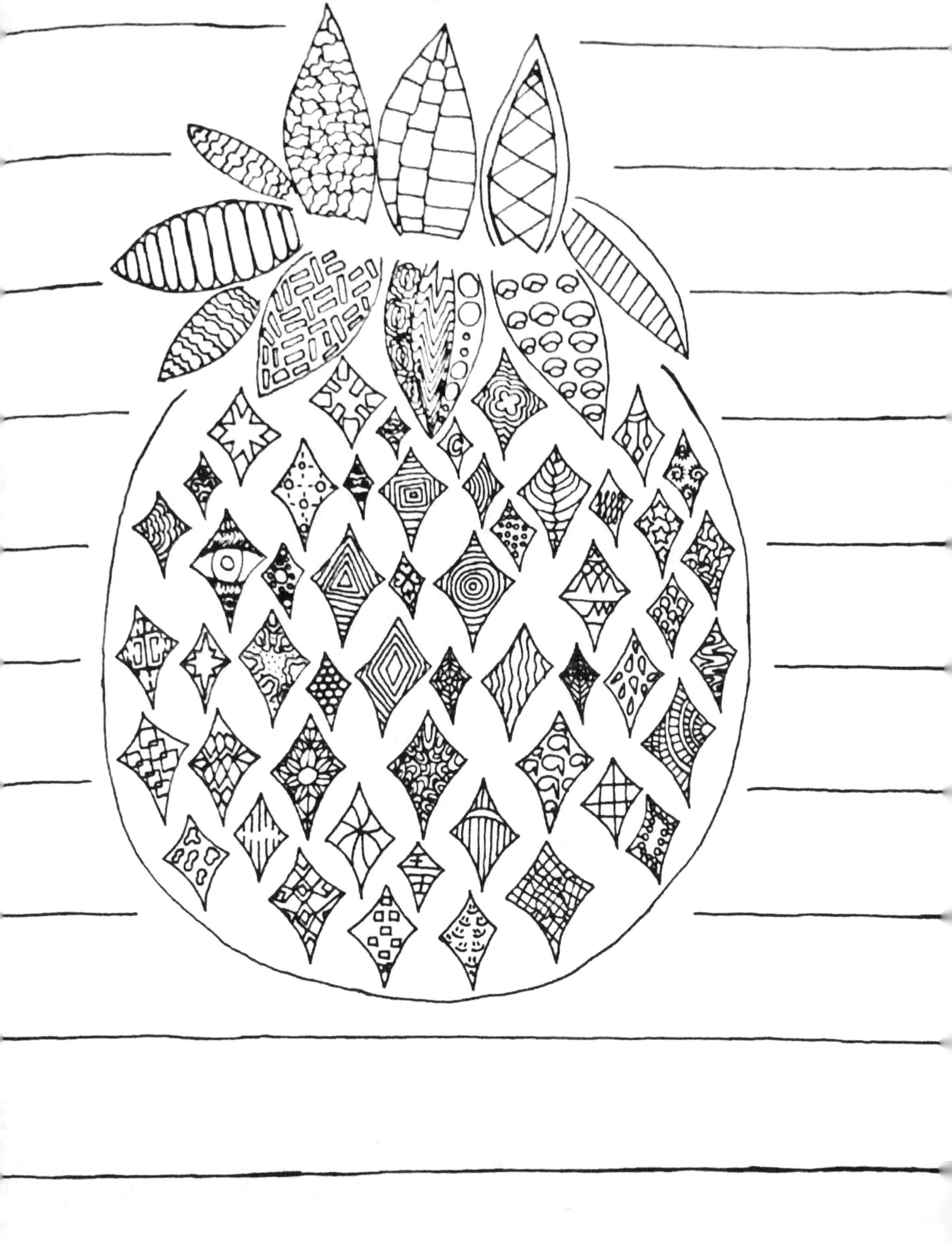

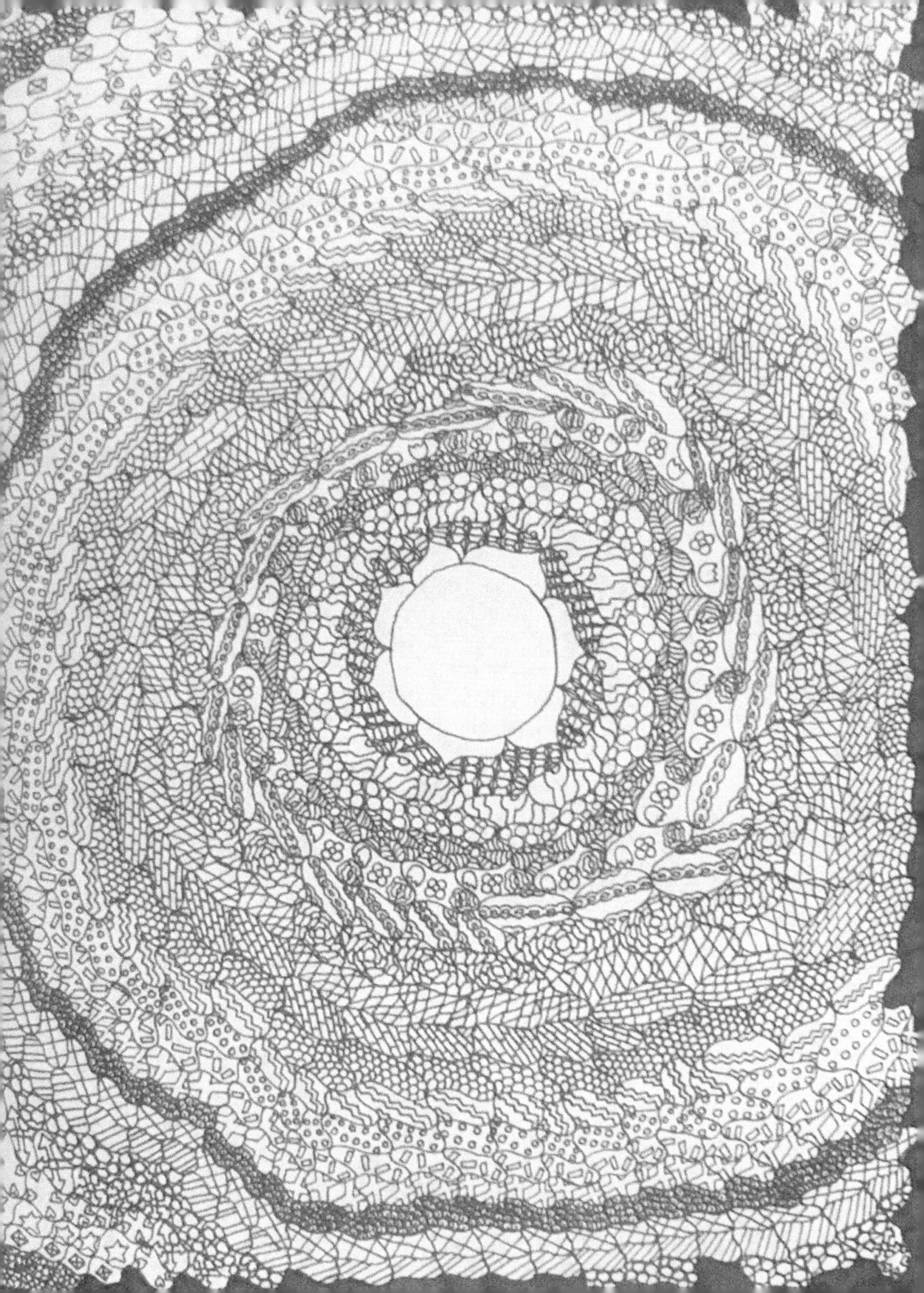

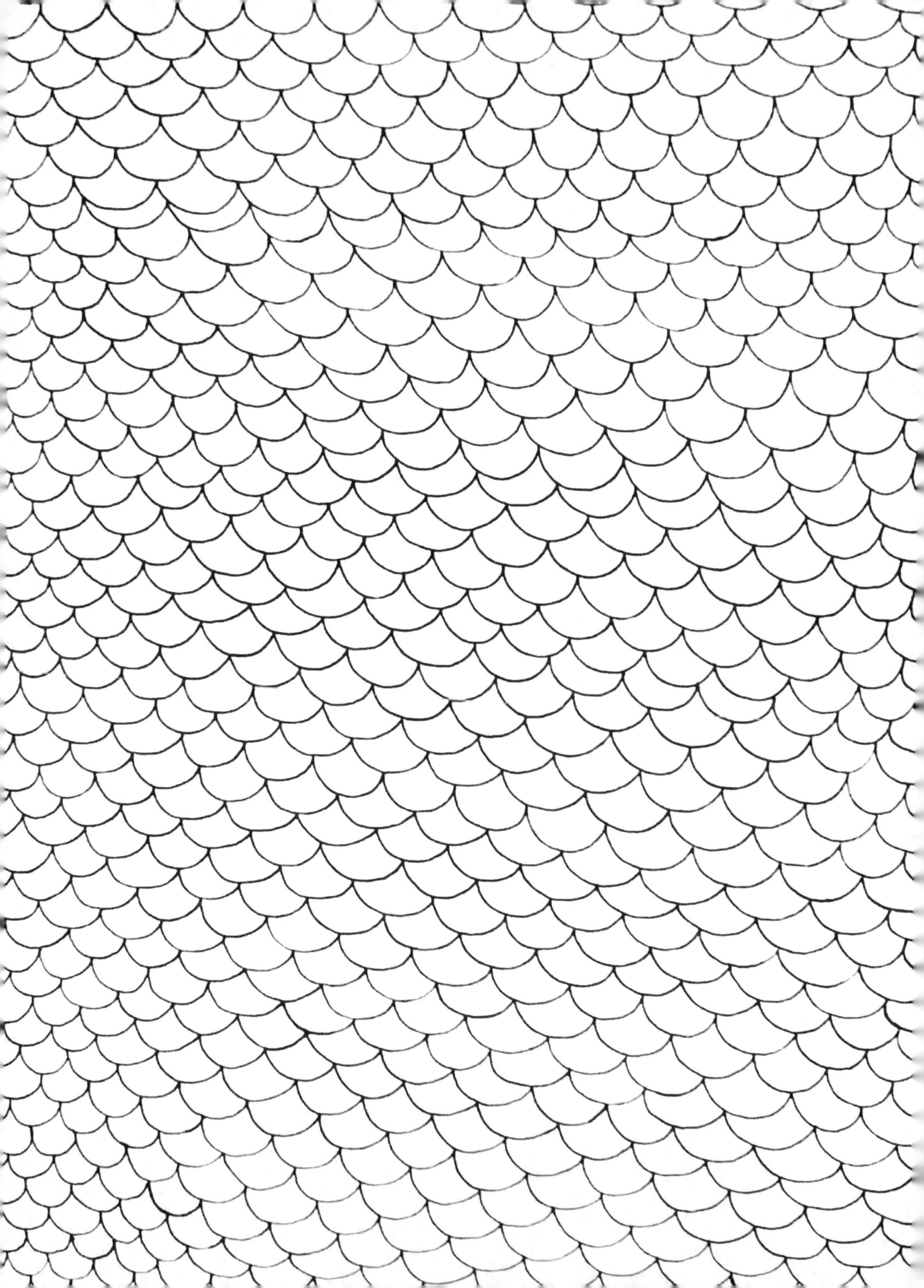

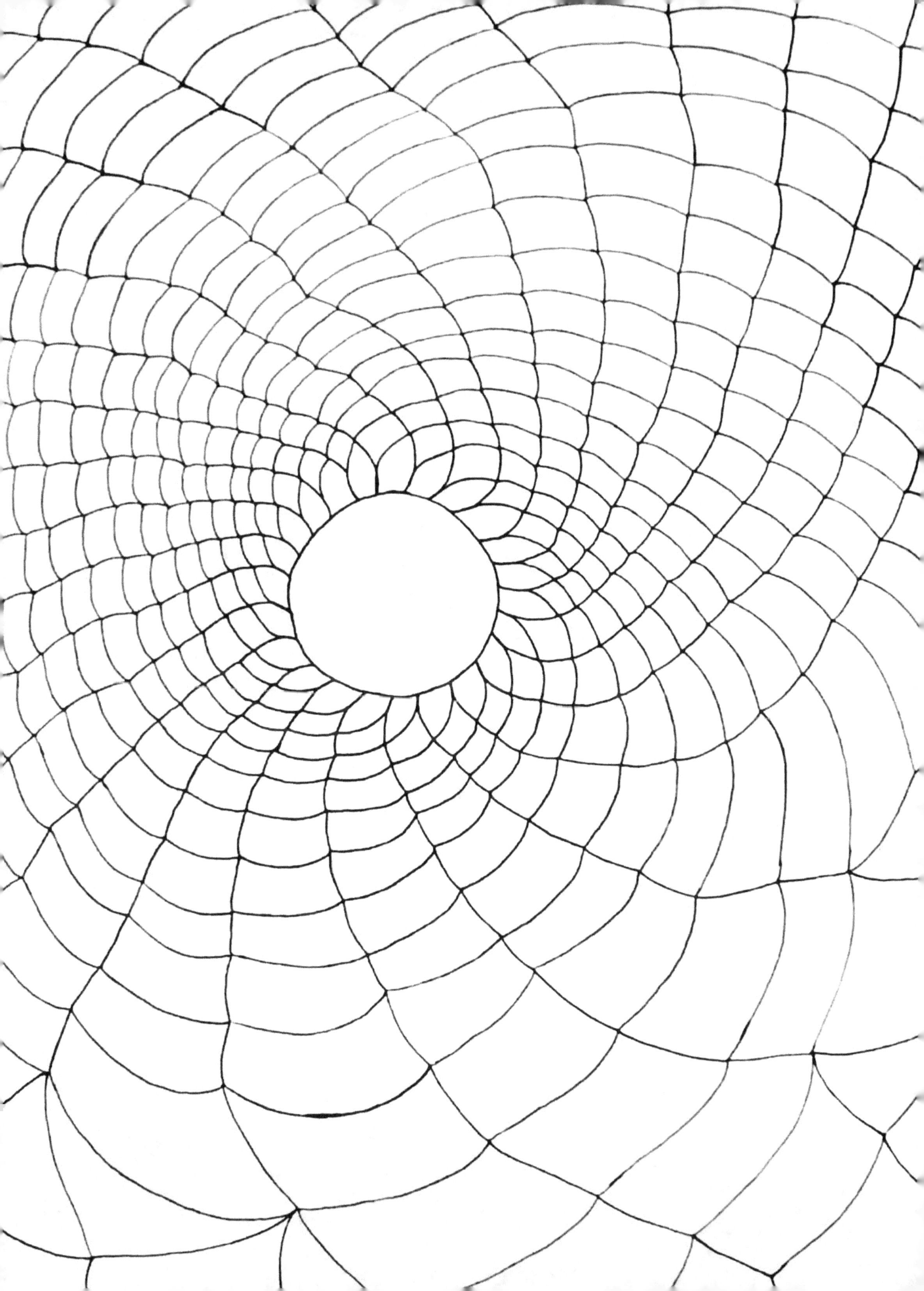

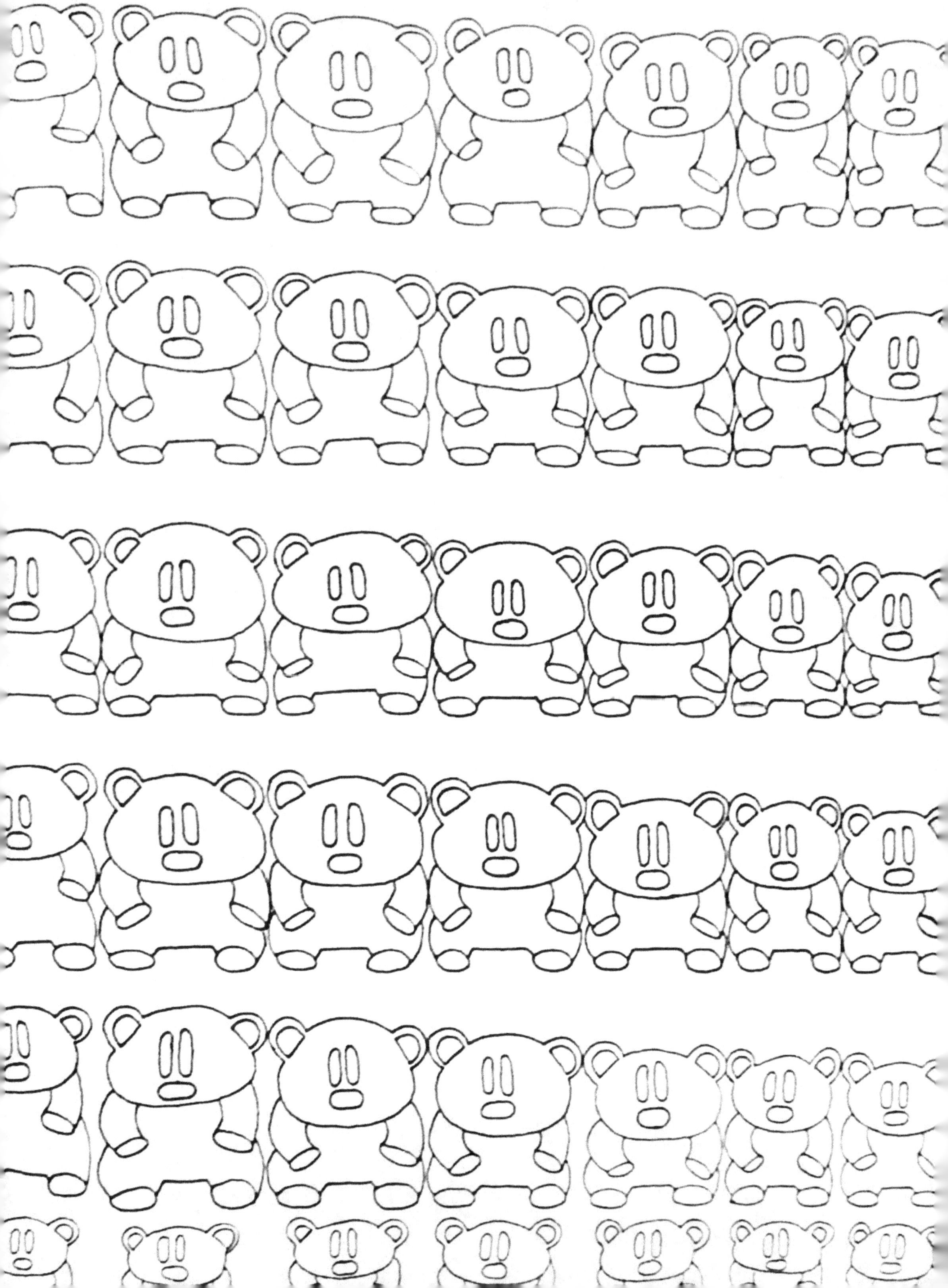

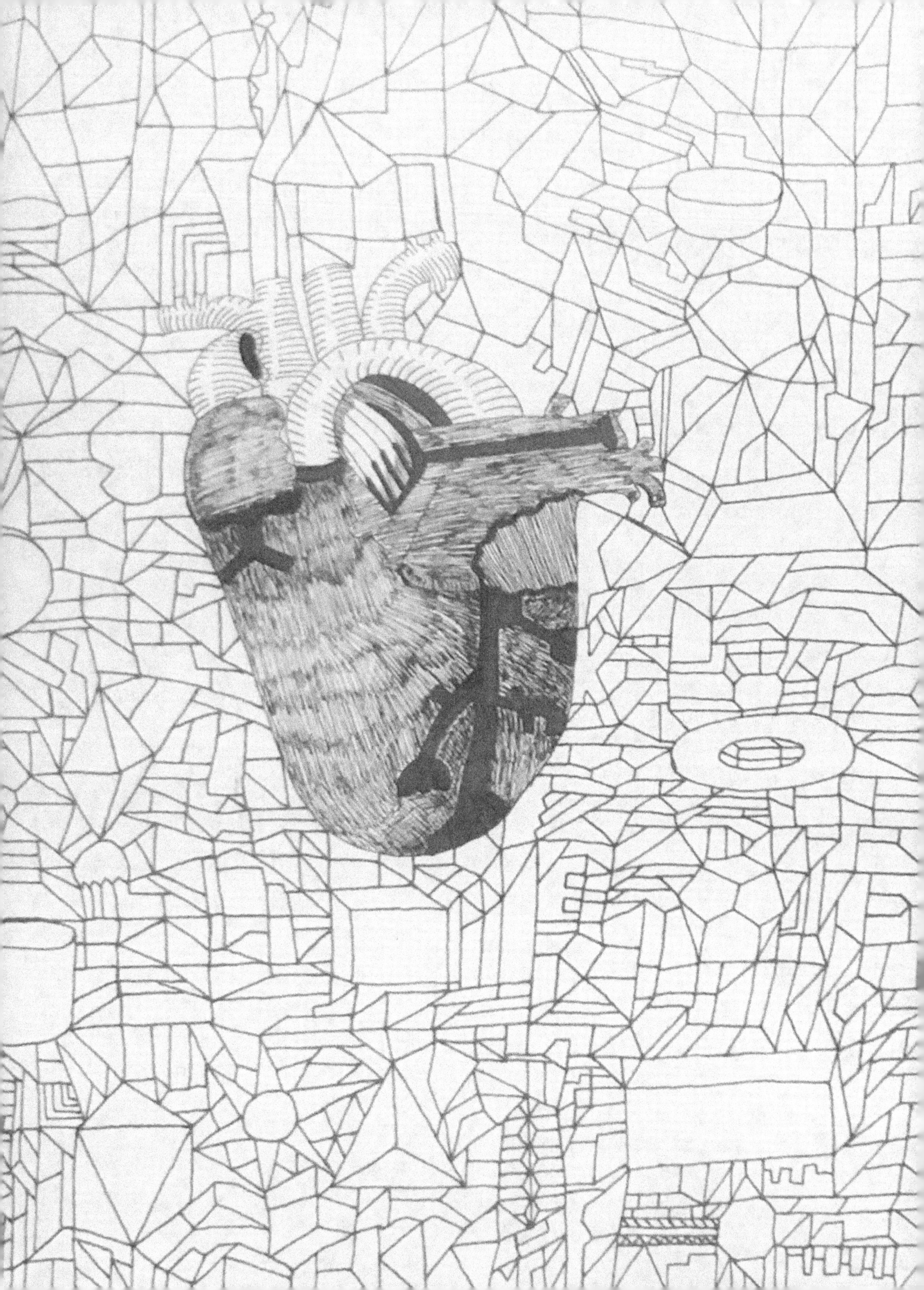

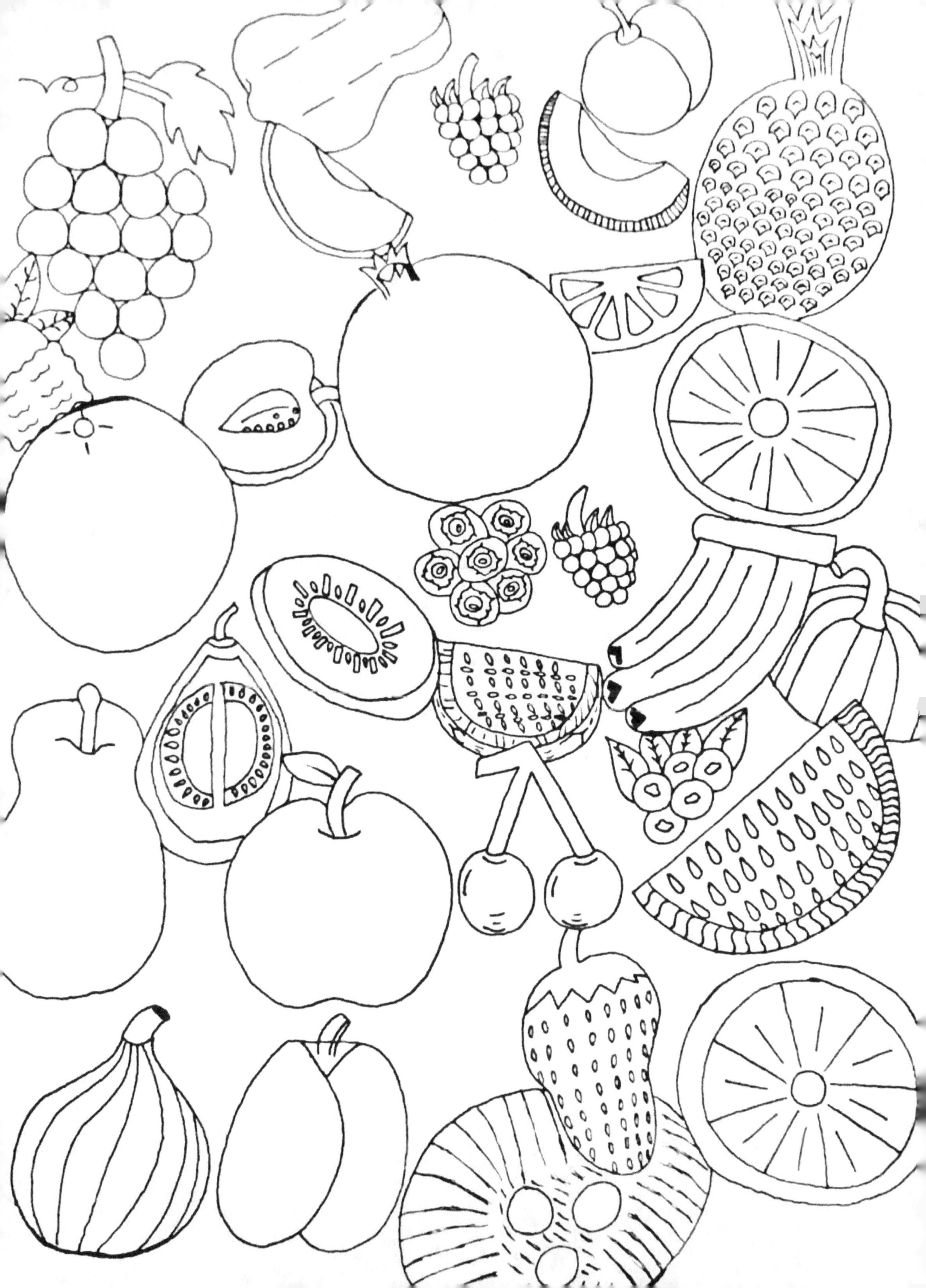

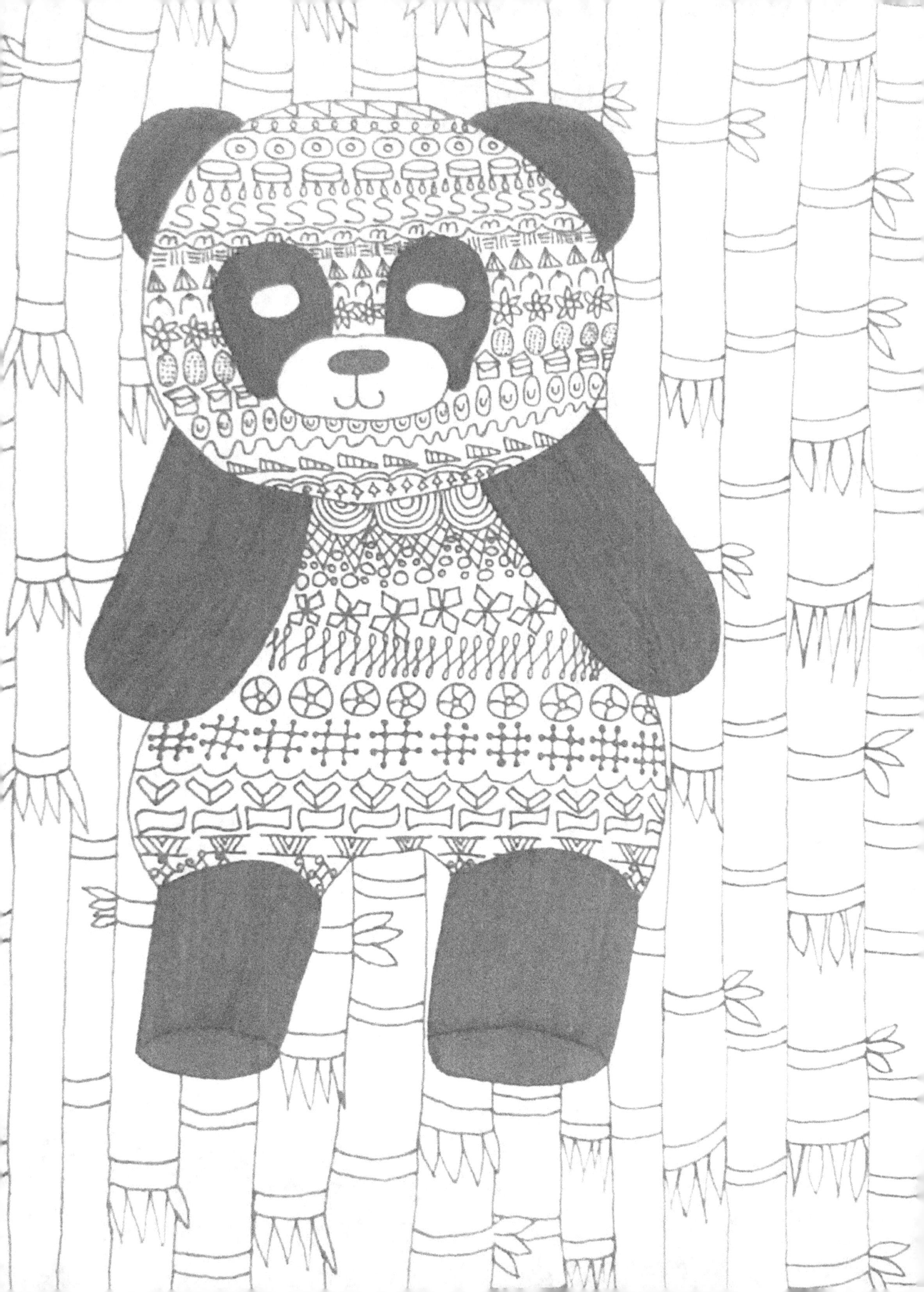

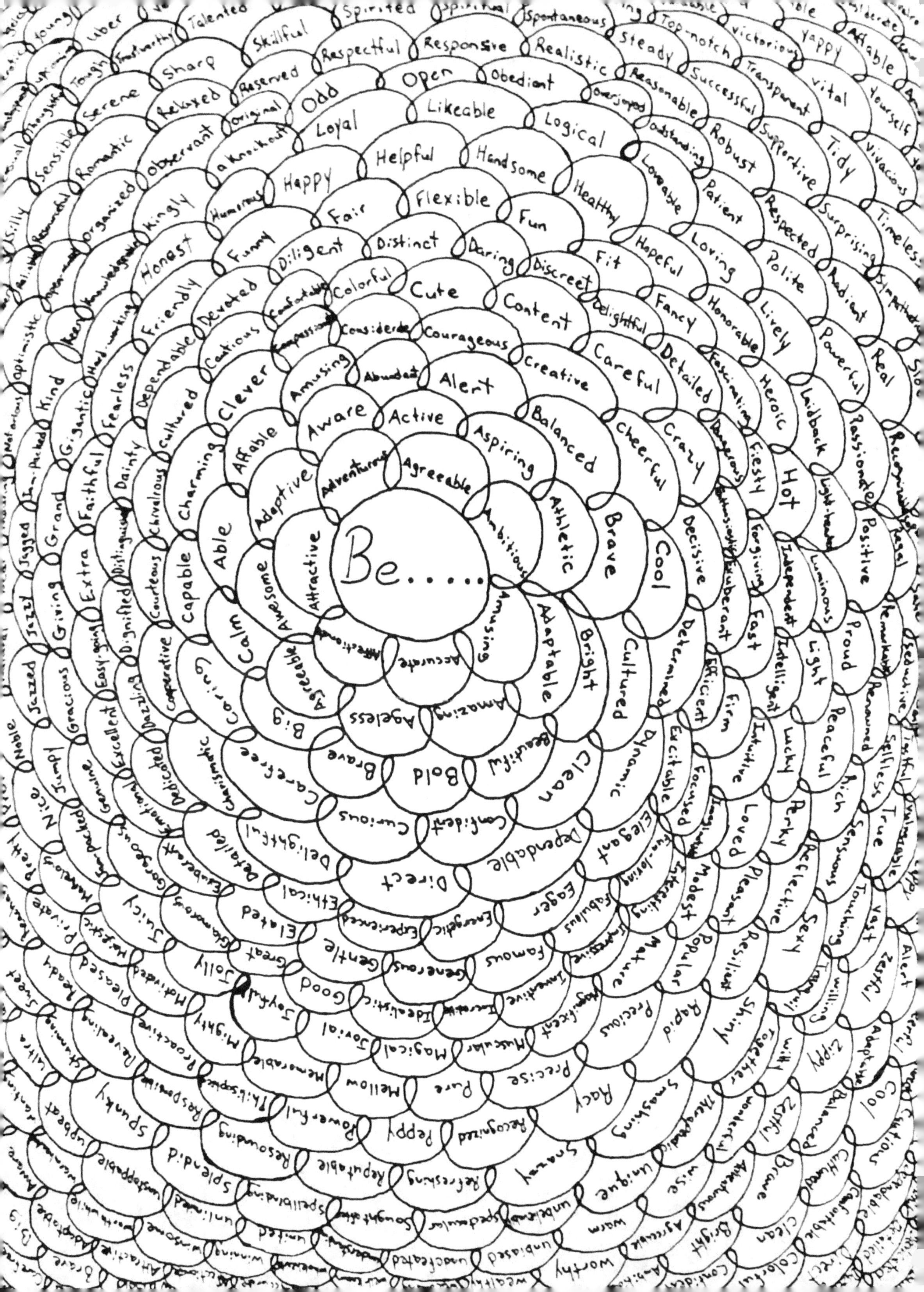
Be.....
Agreeable
Adventurous
Ambitious
Athletic
Attractive
Awesome
Amusing
Adaptable
Accurate
Affectionate
Adaptive
Aware
Active
Aspiring
Balanced
Brave
Cool
Cultured
Bright
Amazing
Ageless
Big
Calm
Able
Affable
Alert
Amusing
Creative
Clever
Charming
Capable
Caring
Carefree
Brave
Bold
Beautiful
Clean
Dynamic
Curious
Confident
Dependable
Direct
Delightful
Cheerful
Crazy
Decisive
Fast
Determined
Efficient
Careful
Detailed
Content
Cute
Colorful
Courageous
Considerate
Cautious
Devoted
Diligent
Distinct
Daring
Discreet
Friendly
Dependable
Faithful
Dainty
Courteous
Cooperative
Dignified
Dazzling
Dedicated
Charismatic
Detailed
Ethical
Elated
Energetic
Experienced
Eager
Elegant
Fun-loving
Focused
Excitable
Firm
Intuitive
Loved
Lucky
Perky
Fit
Fun
Flexible
Fair
Funny
Happy
Helpful
Handsome
Healthy
Hopeful
Fancy
Honorable
Heroic
Hot
Independent
Intelligent
Light
Peaceful
Rich
Sensuous
Proud
Positive
Luminous
Powerful
Real
Lively
Polite
Radiant
Loving
Patient
Respected
Loveable
Logical
Likeable
Open
Obedient
Odd
Loyal
Humorous
Kingly
Honest
Fearless
Kind
Gigantic
Grand
Extra
Giving
Gracious
Excellent
Genuine
Nice
Noble
Jazzed
Jazzy
Jagged
Jumpy
Juicy
Jolly
Great
Glamorous
Gentle
Generous
Famous
Fabulous
Modest
Mature
Popular
Pleasant
Resilient
Reflective
Sexy
Touching
Vast
True
Selfless
Good
Joyful
Idealistic
Jovial
Magical
Muscular
Memorable
Mellow
Pure
Precise
Precious
Rapid
Shiny
Racy
Smashing
Powerful
Peppy
Recognized
Resounding
Reputable
Refreshing
Snazzy
Unique
Splendid
Spunky
Pleased
Mighty
Proactive
Responsive
Private
Pretty
Sweet
Ready
Organized
Romantic
Sensible
Serene
Relaxed
Reserved
Observant
Original
Sharp
Skillful
Talented
Respectful
Responsive
Realistic
Steady
Spirited
Spiritual
Spontaneous
Top-notch
Victorious
Yappy
Affable
Successful
Transparent
Vital
Reasonable
Robust
Supportive
Tidy
Vivacious
Surprising
Timeless
Wise
Warm
Worthy
Unbiased
Unaffected
Winning
Wholesome
Clean
Bright

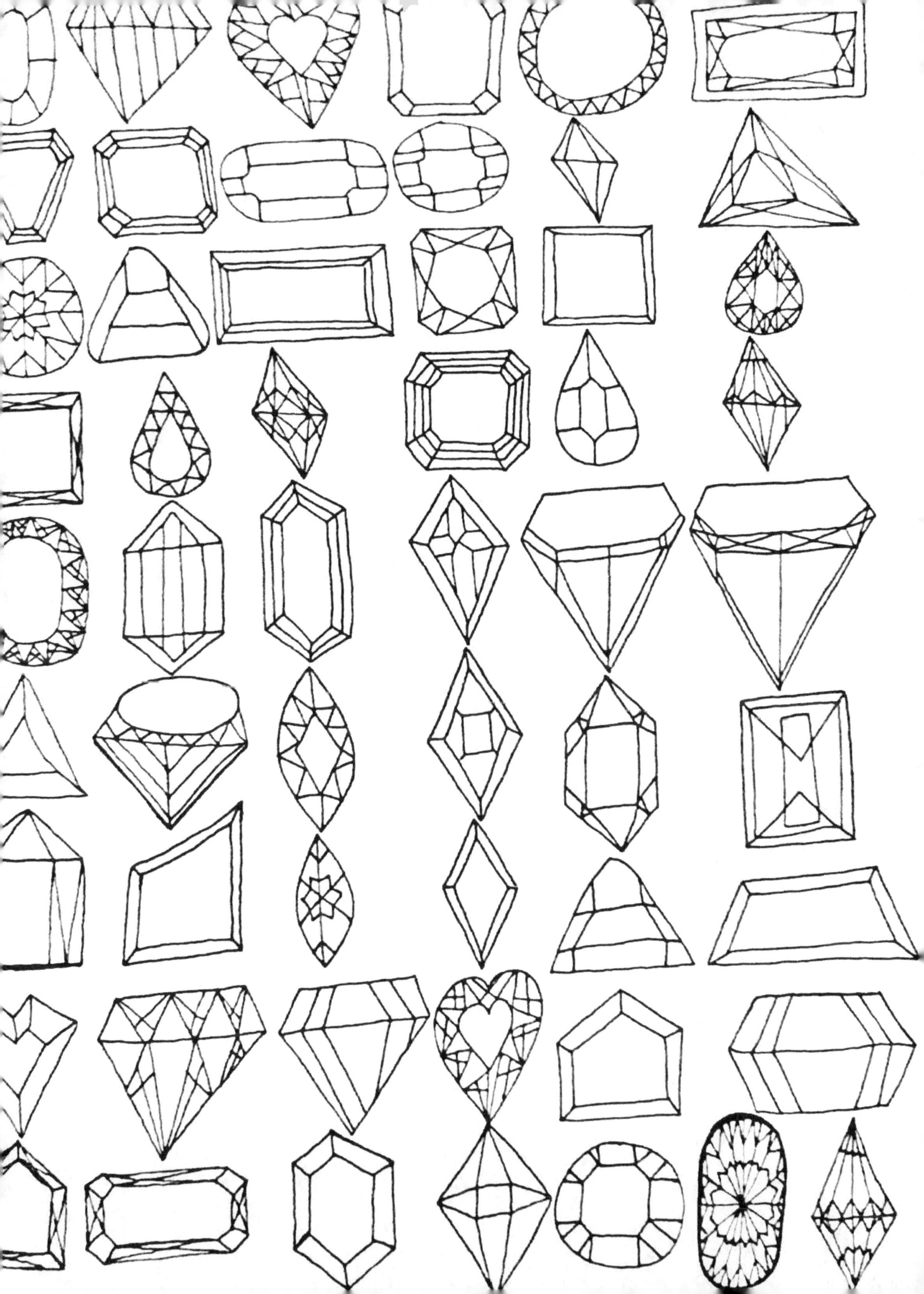

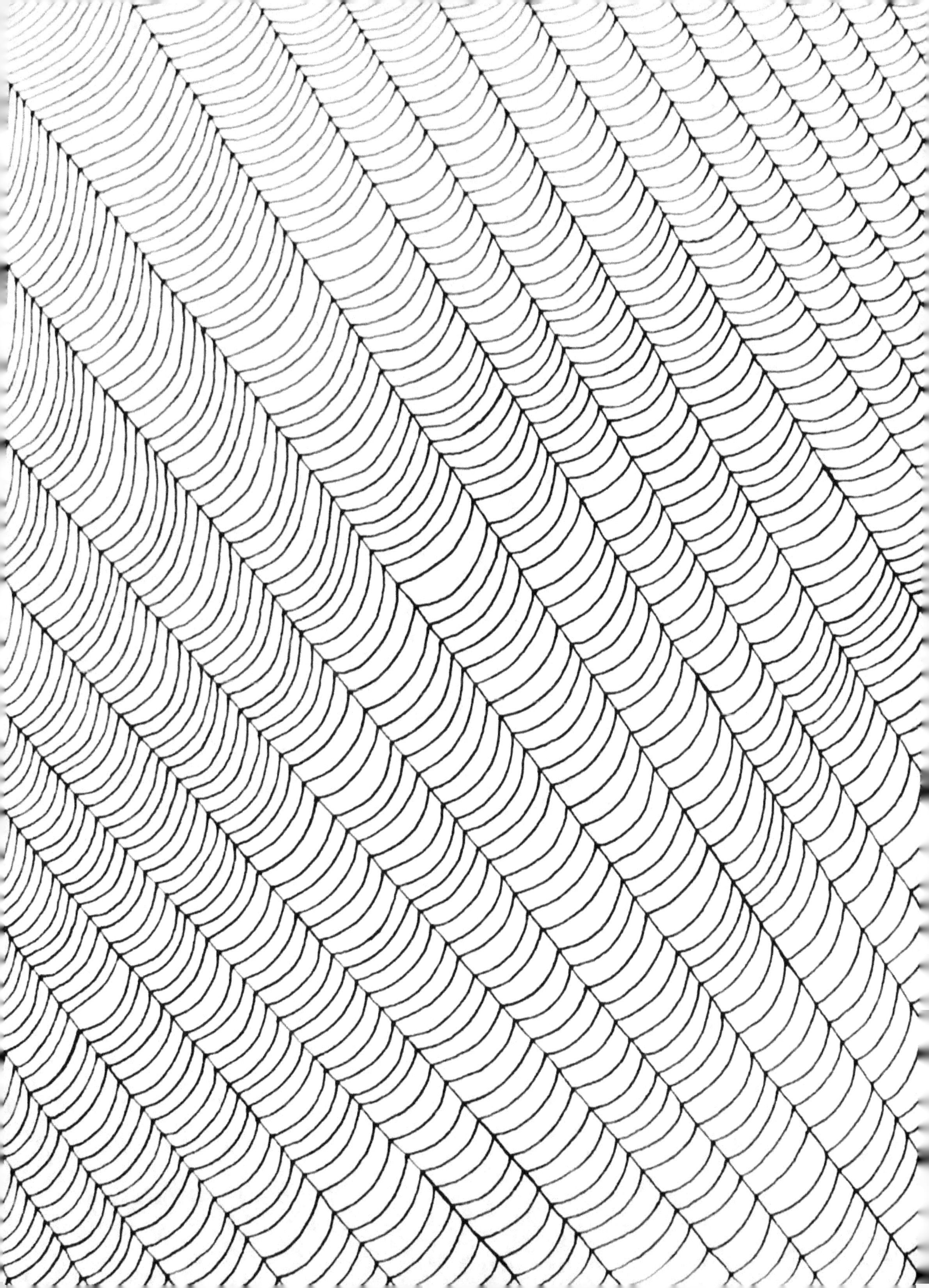

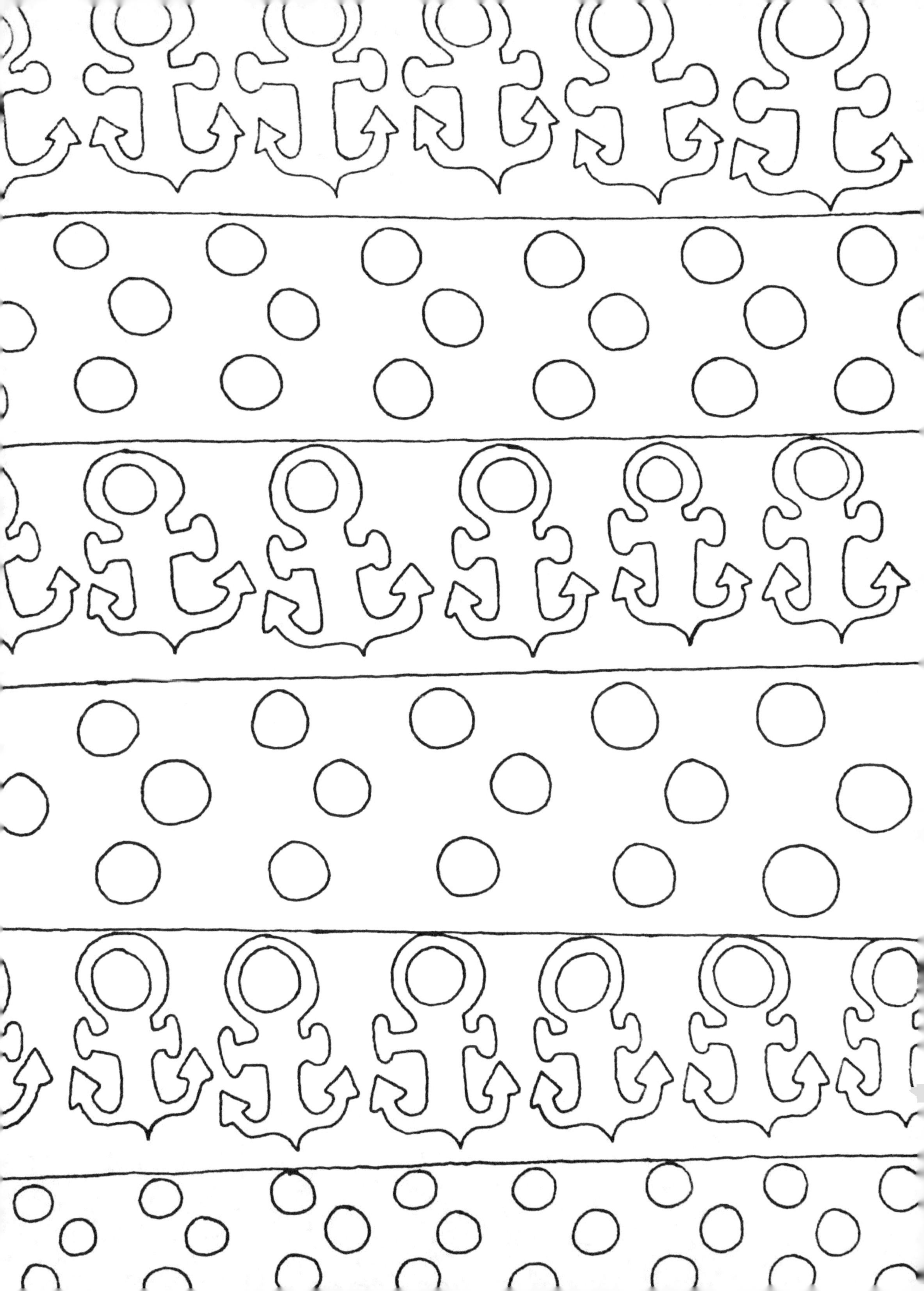

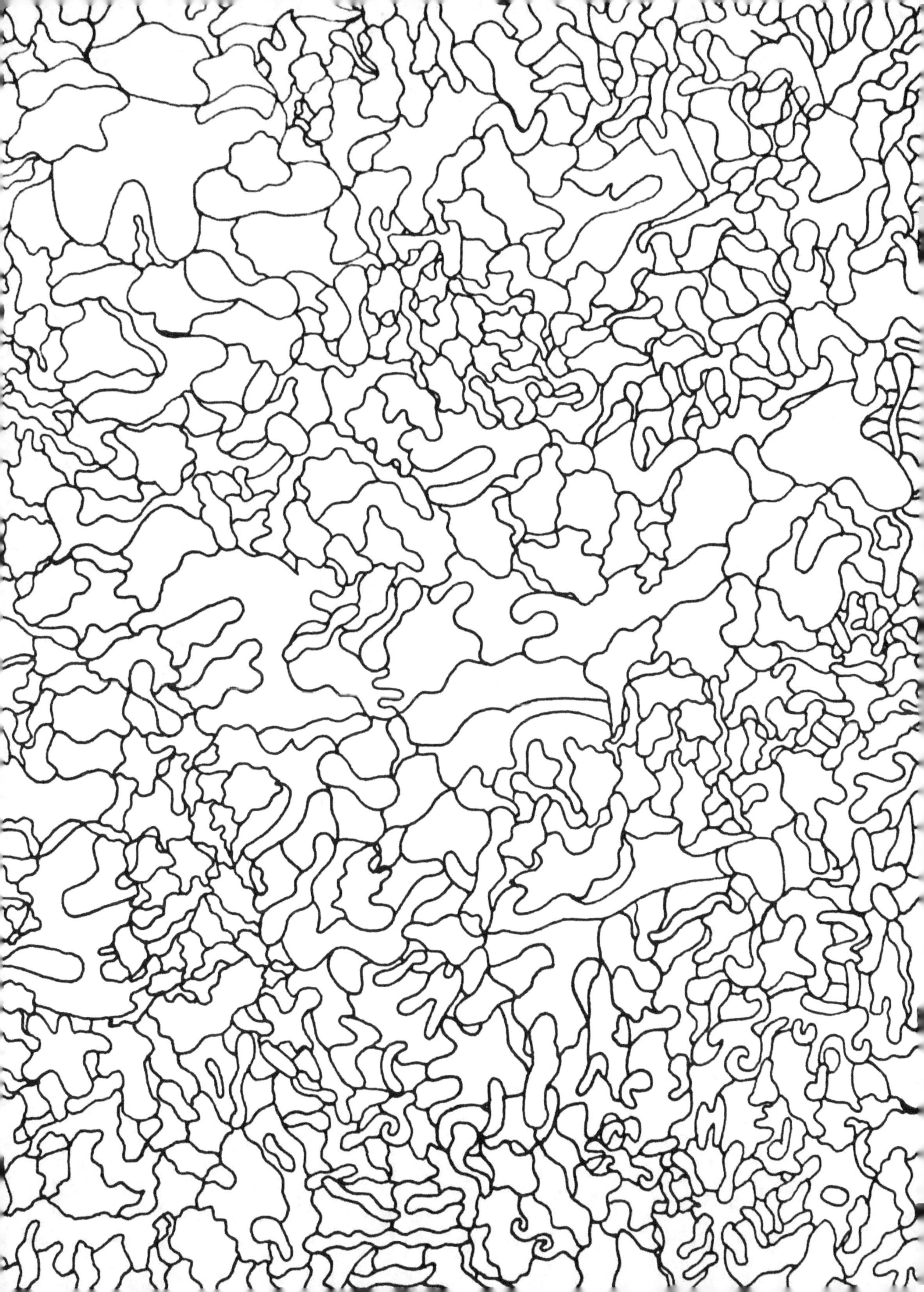

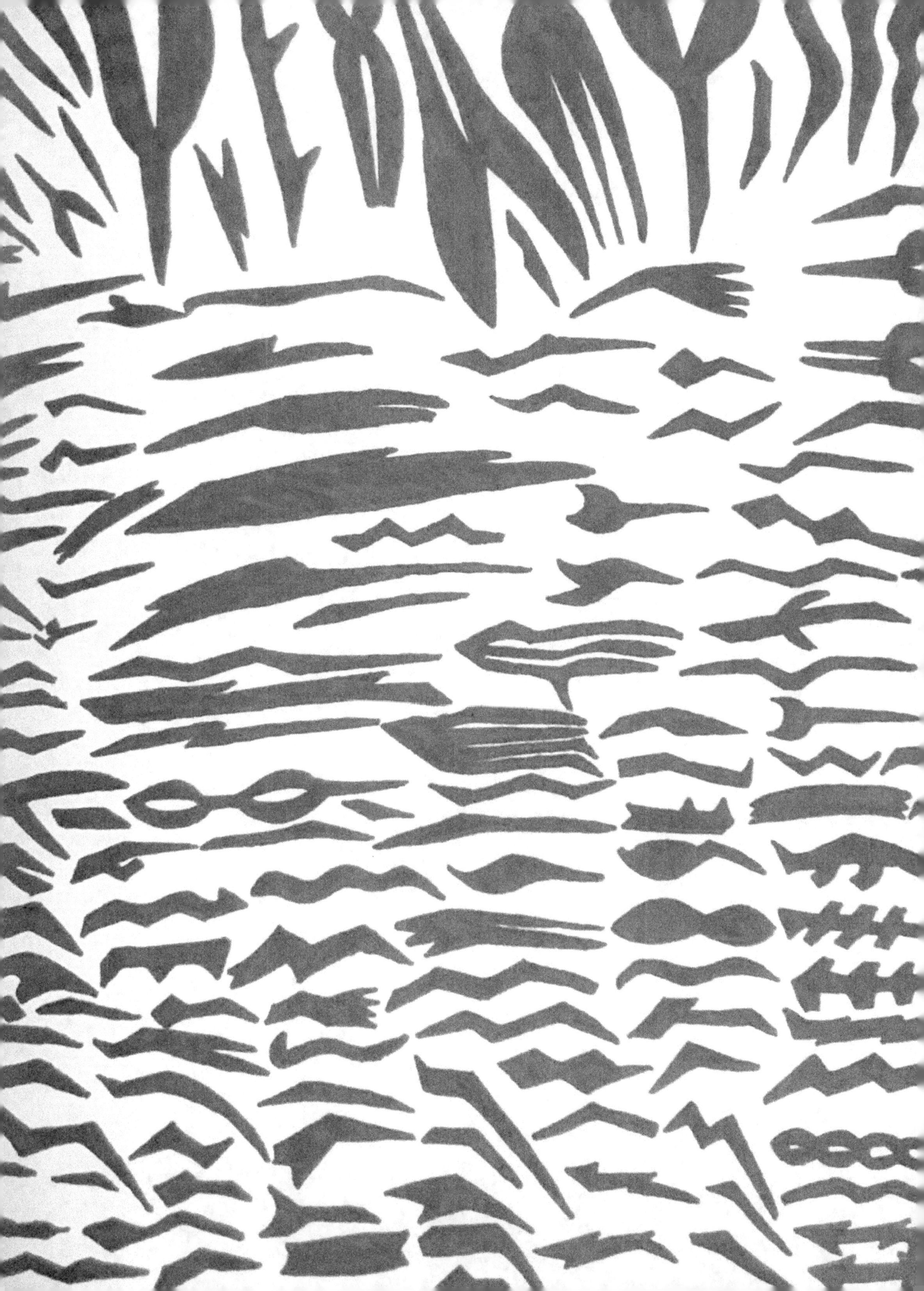

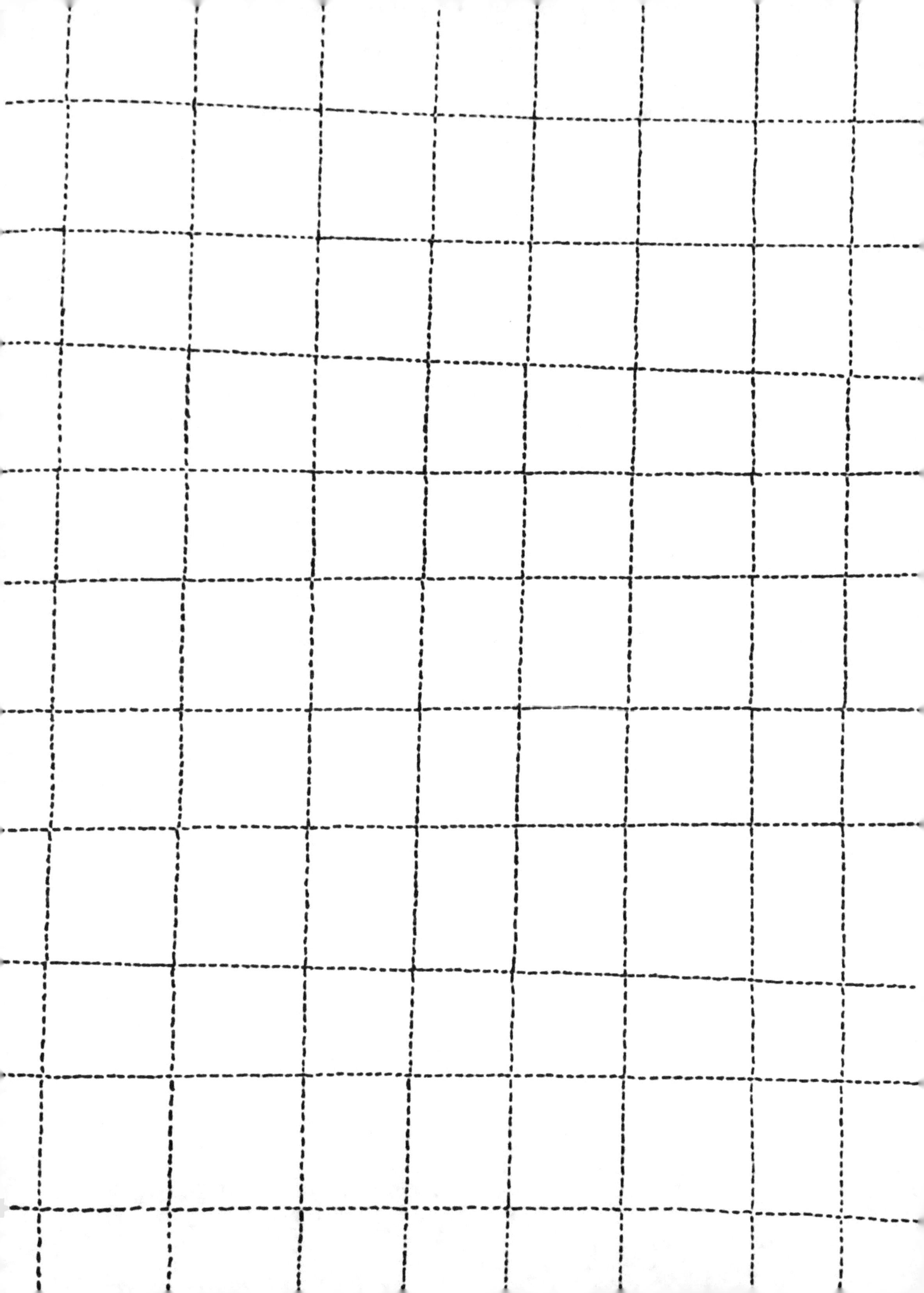

CHIPS
POP CORN
MILK
CHIPS
POP CORN
MILK

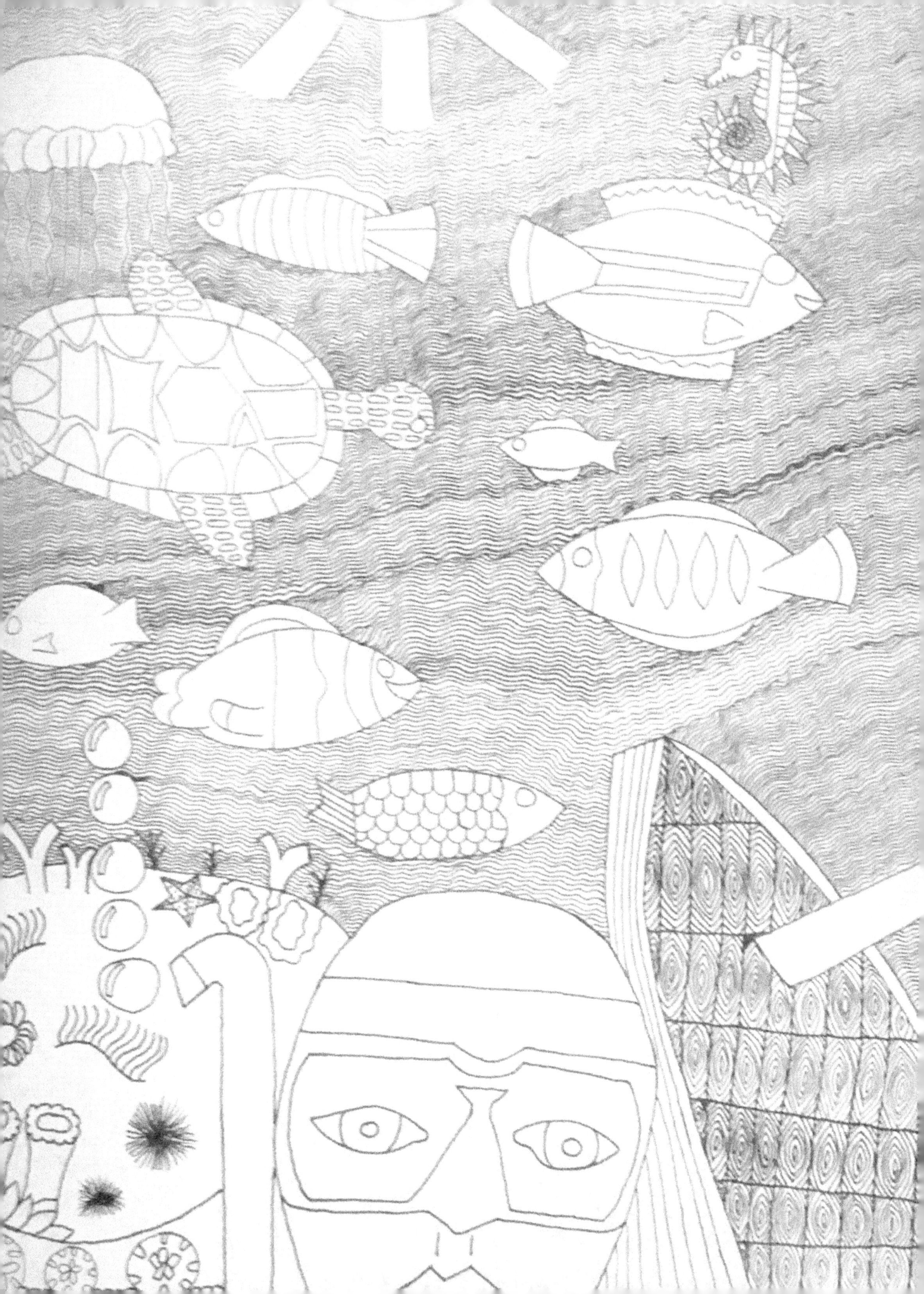

8
1
2
101
1
2
3

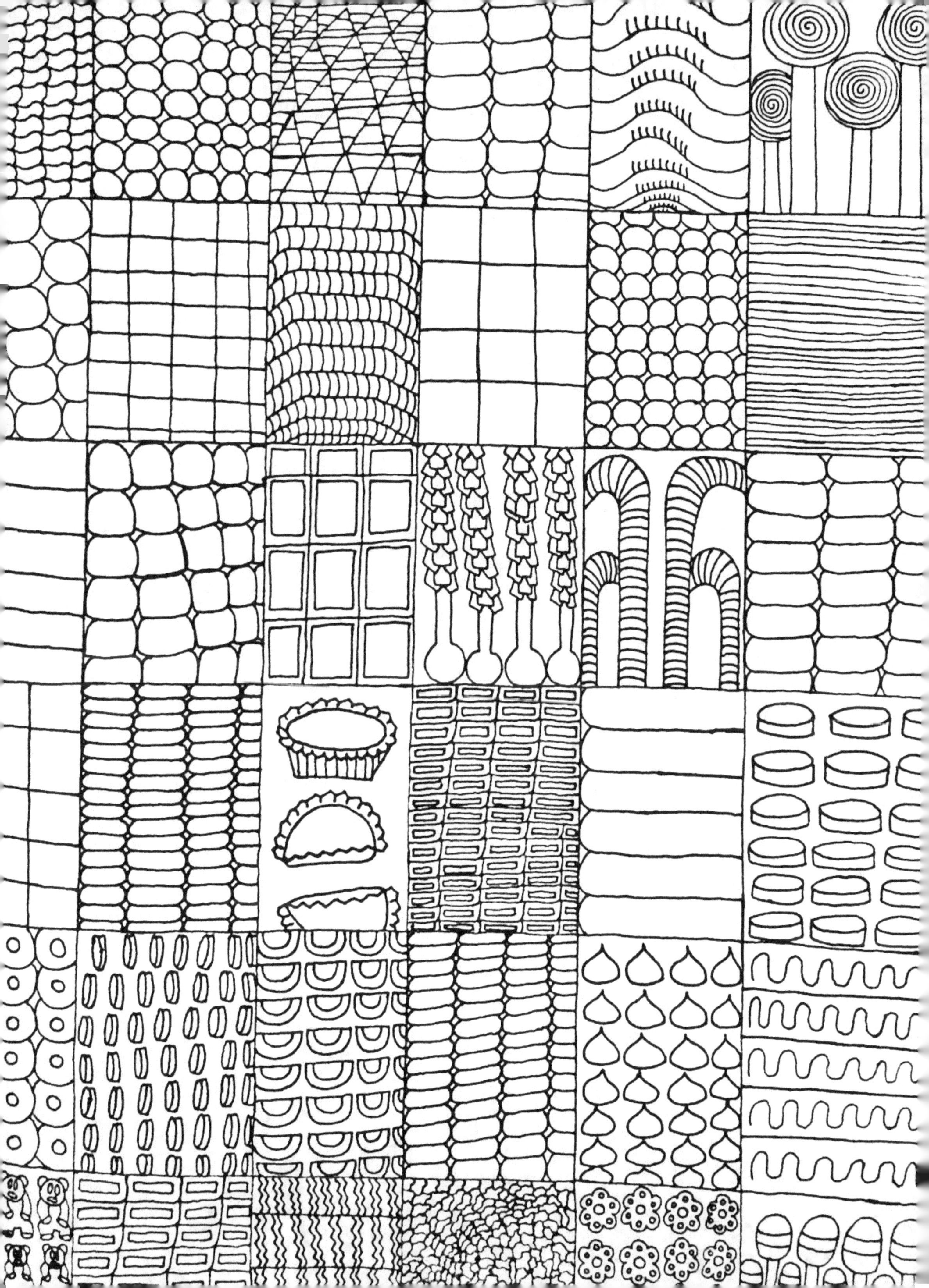

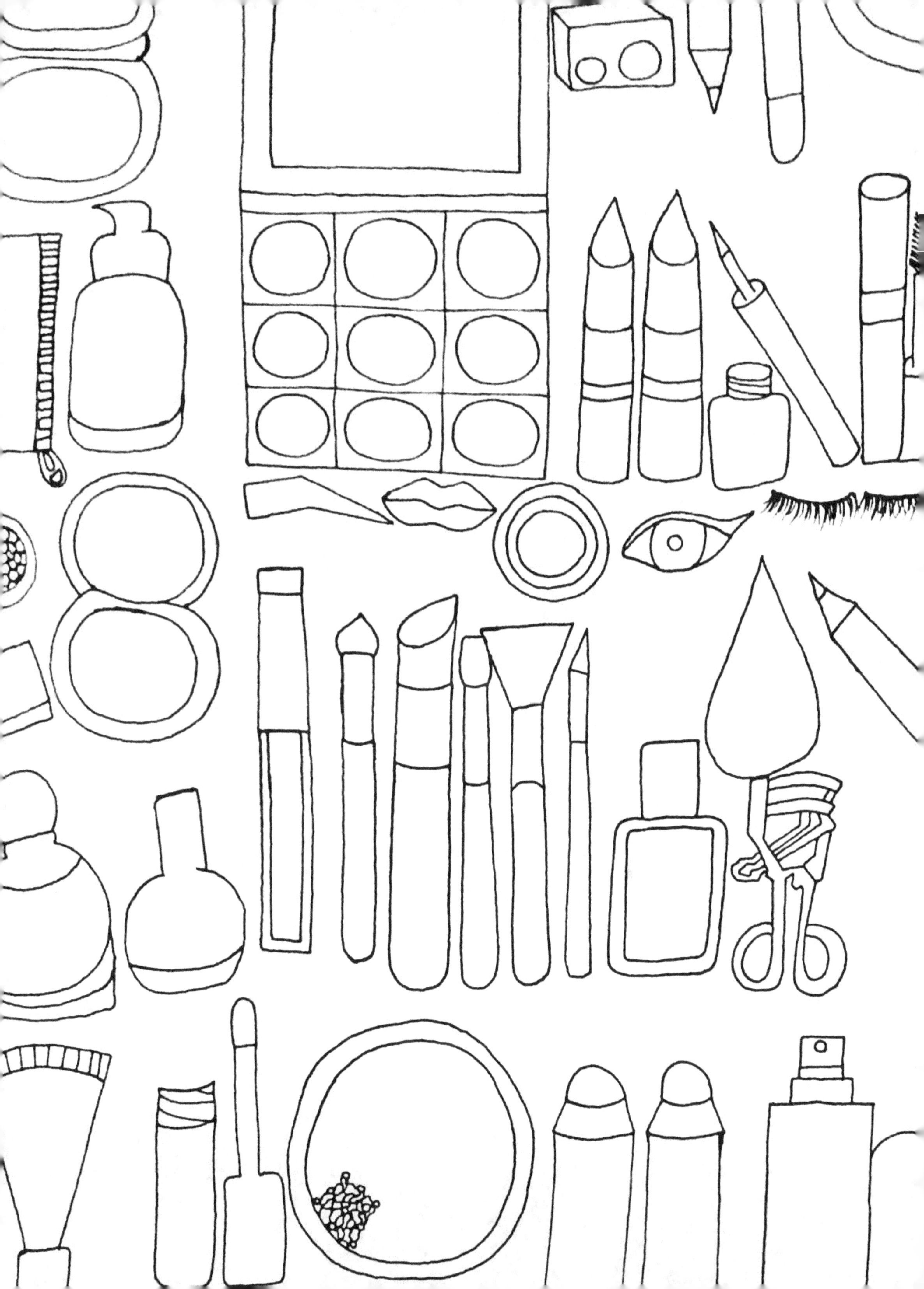

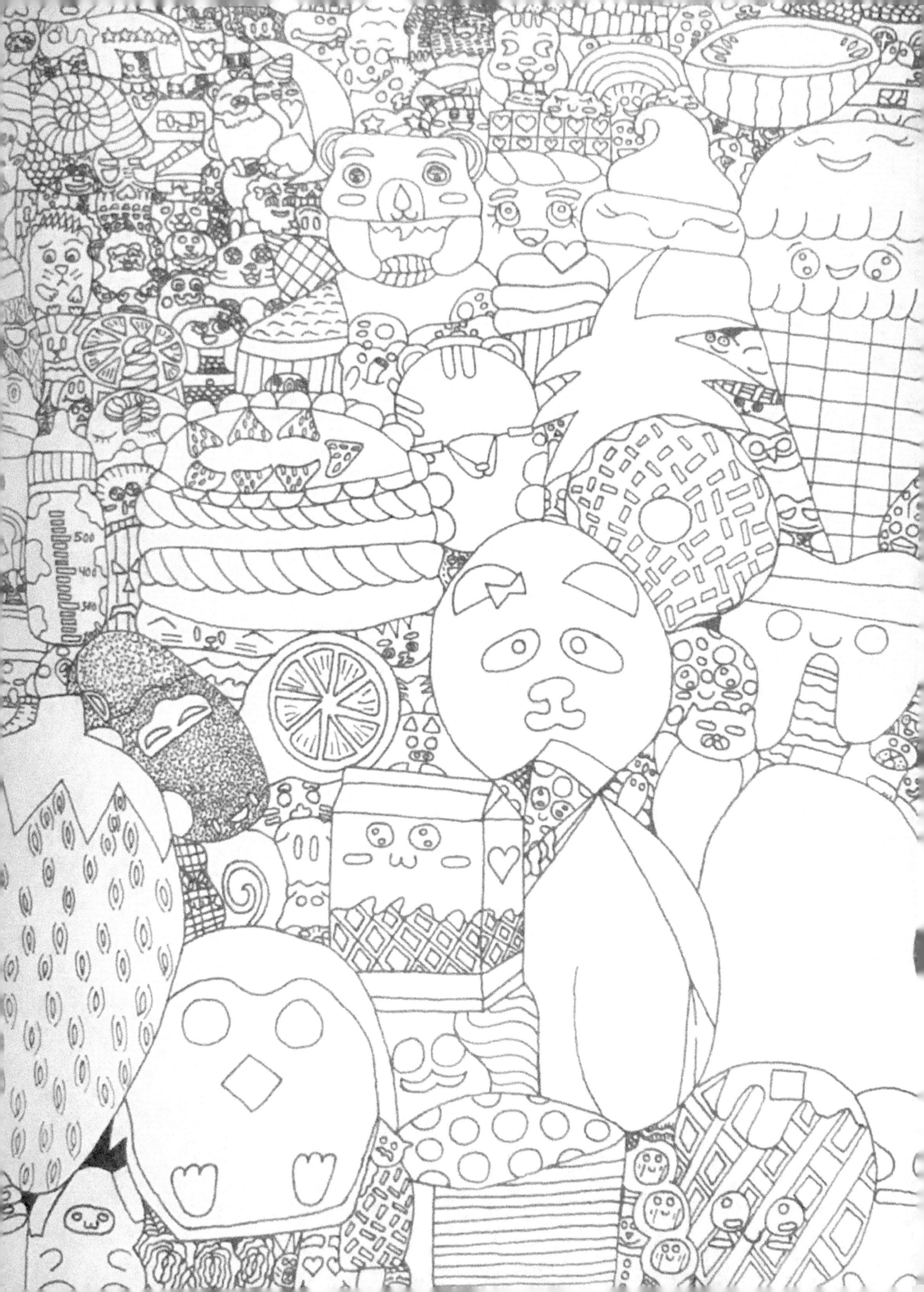
500
400

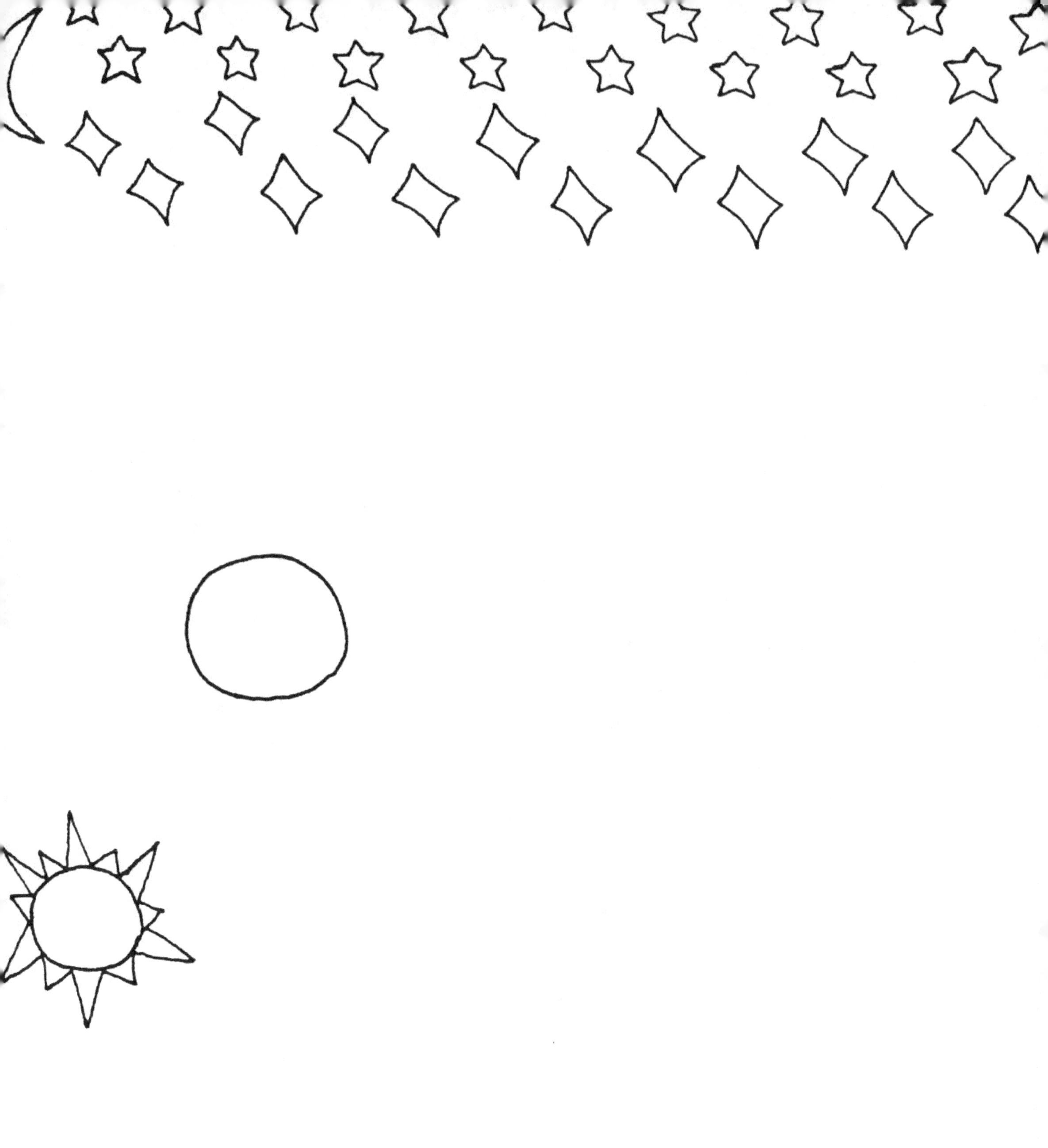

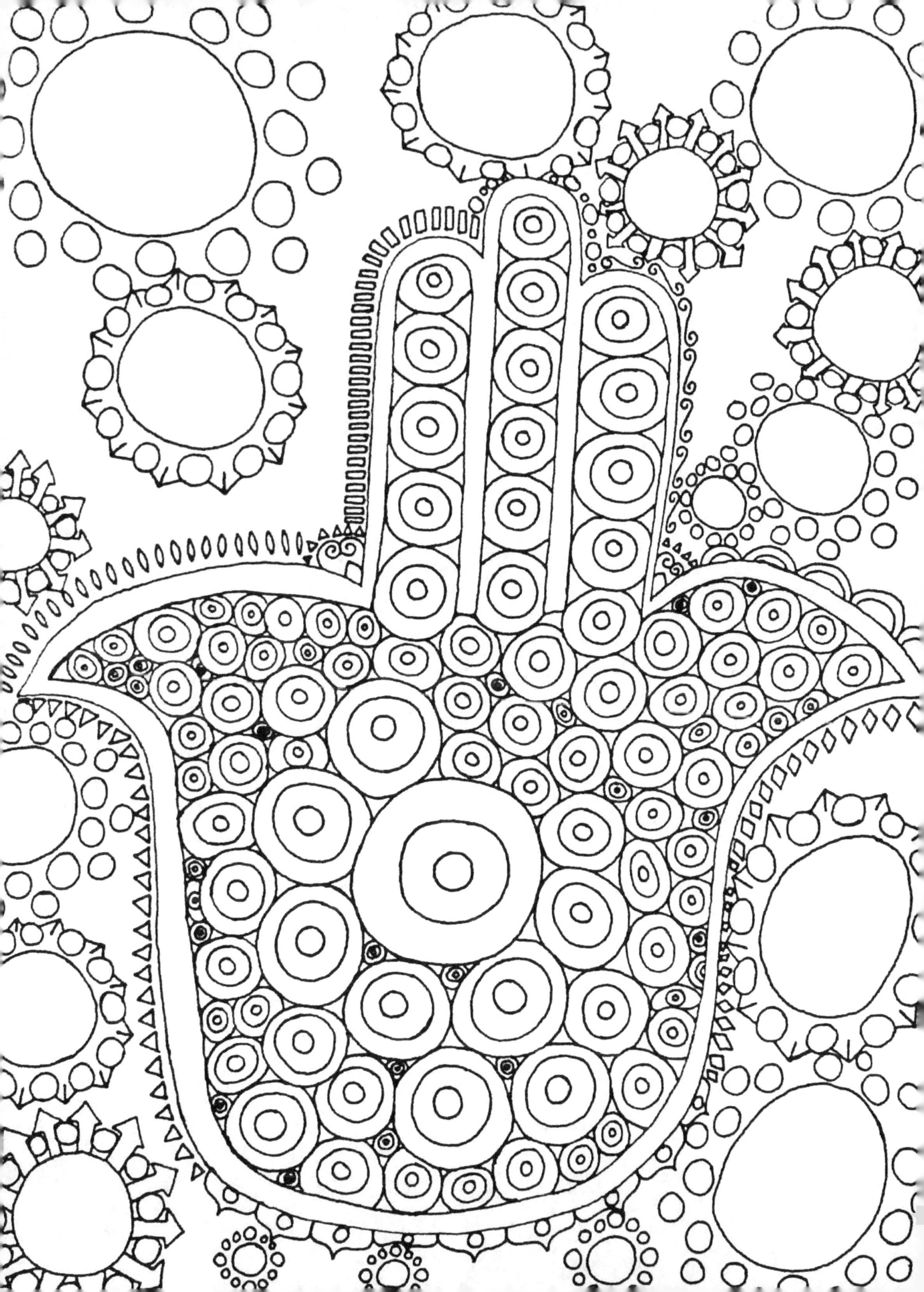

Thanks for Coloring

BE SURE TO SHARE YOUR WORK WITH #makeupthepaige

www.ingramcontent.com/pod-product-compliance
Lightning Source LLC
Chambersburg PA
CBHW081535220526
45467CB00010B/3204
* 9 7 9 8 7 2 9 3 9 9 9 2 5 *